CONQUERING CHAOS AT WORK

Strategies for Managing Disorganization and the People Who Cause It

Harriet Schechter

THE MIRACLE WORKER

Illustrations by Bella Silverstein

A FIRESIDE BOOK

Published by Simon & Schuster

New York   London   Sydney   Singapore

FIRESIDE
Rockefeller Center
1230 Avenue of the Americas
New York, NY 10020

FIRESIDE and colophon are registered trademarks
of Simon & Schuster, Inc.

Designed by Pagesetters

Manufactured in the United States of America

1   3   5   7   9   10   8   6   4   2

Library of Congress Cataloging-in-Publication Data
Schechter, Harriet.
Conquering chaos at work : strategies for managing disorganization
and the people who cause it / Harriet Schechter.
p.   cm.
Includes bibliographical references and index.
1. Organizational effectiveness.   2. Organizational behavior.   I. Title.
HD58.9.S34 2000
658.3'045—dc21   99-047904
ISBN 0-684-86314-6

To my parents,
Bill Schechter and Pauline Jaret Schechter,
with infinite love and appreciation

In all chaos there is a cosmos,
in all disorder a secret order.

—Carl Jung

A Fable

Once upon a time there was a land called Soahc. It looked like a big office filled with many busy people. Some of the people were considerate of others and, thus, conscientious about getting their work done, and some weren't. Those who weren't conscientious created confusion and disorder for everyone else.

Eventually, they overran the land and turned everything topsy-turvy, including its name. Soahc became Chaos, and the people who created Chaos became known as the Chaos Creators. The others, who were conscientious and considerate, gradually weakened, and their numbers were reduced. And so it came to pass that they became the slaves of the Chaos Creators and were forced to clean up the messes that the Chaos Creators continually created.

But one day, when things were looking particularly bleak for the slaves, they got together and said, "Enough!" They looked around them for someone with the courage to lead them out of this desert of disorganization.

"What we need," one of them finally cried, "is a Chaos Conqueror! But who among us has the will and the skill to restore order and consideration? Who cares enough about us and about our work to rescue us from the Chaos Creators?"

Everyone's eyes darted about, looking for that person who would assume the mantle of Chaos Conqueror, who would go throughout the land creating order out of Chaos. And, finally, all their eyes came to rest on . . . you.

Of course, this is a fable. Nothing in it is true.
Except for the part about you becoming a Chaos Conqueror. . . .

Contents

Introduction

*H*as getting organized failed you?

Notice I didn't ask if you've failed to get organized. Mark Twain once wrote that success is the ability to go from failure to failure with great enthusiasm. So according to that definition, as long as you keep trying to get organized, you haven't failed at it. But it may have failed you.

Why? Because chaos does not respect organization. Chaos will happen no matter how tidy you keep your desk and no matter how carefully you organize your files. Chaos can occur as quick as a crash-causing keystroke or as slow as a meaningless meeting. It slips into your day via last-minute cancellations, forgotten deadlines, and unreturned phone calls. To paraphrase a famous saying, "Chaos is what happens when you're making other plans."

Think about all the times you've tried to get more organized. Perhaps you read a book that gave you tips such as "handle each piece of paper only once" and "a place for everything and everything in its place." Maybe you attended a seminar on time management, or listened to a tape that told you how to set up a new filing system.

But does any of this traditional organizing wisdom help you when your boss habitually dumps "due yesterday" projects on your desk? Or your coworkers keep borrowing materials they forget to return? Or your assistant can't find the file you gave him or her this morning? Or your most important client repeatedly reschedules appointments at the last minute?

Getting organized probably isn't enough to save you from these and other types of chaos—because it addresses only one of three possible chaos conduits.

◆◆◆

Chaos Clarification

Chaos means different things to different people. So right now, let's avoid confusion by getting clear about what chaos means in this book. Chaos is a disruptive consequence of people's disorganized and/or inconsiderate actions or inactions. It is not used here merely as a synonym for clutter, change, or commotion.

◆◆◆

Putting Chaos in Context

In your workplace, chaos usually comes from at least one of the following sources:

1. The chaos you create for yourself.
2. The chaos you create for others (which can boomerang back to you).
3. The chaos others create for you.

Getting organized only addresses the first, and possibly the second, sources of chaos—but not the third. That's why this book is unique. It will show you how to manage all types of workplace chaos, no matter what—or who—is the source: your boss, your coworkers, your assistant, your clients . . . or yourself.

You are about to discover how you can transform yourself from a Chaos Creator (or the victim of Chaos Creators) into a Chaos Conqueror. A Chaos Conqueror is someone who goes beyond being well-organized—because in today's workplace, organized just isn't enough. You need to know how to dismantle chaos bombs before they explode, instead of just cleaning up the mess afterward.

The process of becoming a Chaos Conqueror involves learning how to recognize the roots of chaos as well as how to identify recurring chaos patterns. This will enable you to anticipate chaos so you can avoid it, minimize its impact, counteract it, or work with it.

Chaos Creators and Chaos Conquerors

Conquering Chaos at Work is basically about two kinds of people: those who often cause chaos—Chaos Creators; and those who consistently counteract it—Chaos Conquerors.

Chaos Creators usually create chaos through *reactive* behavior and lack of planning. Chaos Conquerors conquer chaos *proactively* by anticipating it, identifying its sources, and strategizing.

This book will teach you how to identify and understand the first group and how to join the ranks of the second.

How can you learn to do this—especially if you're still struggling with your own disorganization?

I'm going to teach you how.

Out of Chaos Comes . . . This Book

Since 1986, when I founded The Miracle Worker Organizing Service in San Diego, California, I've helped hundreds of people and businesses get organized. Working hands-on with clients who are immersed in varying degrees of chaos, I've discovered the most effective ways of developing and enhancing a person's latent organizational skills.

Over the years, as I spoke to thousands more via seminars and workshops, I began to notice a pattern. More and more people were asking (sometimes begging!) for advice on how to handle the chaos created by someone else's disorganization, not just their own. Bosses were complaining about their disorganized assistants, assistants moaned about their chaos-causing bosses, coworkers blamed their colleagues for ongoing mess-ups, business owners griped about disorderly employees, consultants told tales of chaotic clients—and eventually, this book was born.

The trade secrets in this book are real-life solutions, tried and tested techniques and tools from my years as an organizing consultant. The anecdotes and case histories are true; the names and certain details have been changed, however, to protect the organizationally impaired.

Which Kind of Person Are You?

Some people are born with the organizing gene. As youngsters, they keep their toys and games in order without needing to be nagged. In school, their notebooks never have dog-eared pages sticking out in every direction, and you can always count on them to actually have a copy of the class syllabus that the teacher handed out on the first day of school. Once in the workforce, these people consistently make deadlines, keep appointments, and honor commitments.

For others, though, being organized doesn't come naturally. Instead, they have to really work at it. In childhood, they are the ones who clean up their rooms only after parental prodding; in school, they may have to struggle to get their assignments turned in on time. But they still manage to muddle through. When they hit the workplace, they learn how to do the best they can, making ongoing efforts to stay on top of their workloads.

Then there's a third group: the people who turn their disorganization into almost an art form. As kids, their rooms may be such disasters that their parents don't even bother to nag them anymore. In school, they routinely lose their homework, often turn in projects that may appear fine but are actually incomplete, and invariably manage to come up with excuses for not getting things done (such as the classic "my dog ate it"). By the time they enter the workforce, these folks have developed habits that create chaos not only for themselves but for practically anyone with whom they interact. I call them Chaos Creators.

◆◆

Gifts and Gaps

We all have gifts and we all have gaps. If you weren't born with the gift of organization, you probably have other gifts (or at least abilities). But your talents may be unrecognized or undervalued if they are continually overshadowed by your chaos-causing gaps.

◆◆

What is a Chaos Creator?

A Chaos Creator isn't just someone who continually misplaces files, usually runs late, or regularly forgets things. Those are just symptoms of disorganization. And being disorganized does not alone create chaos for oneself or others. If a disorganized person usually manages to respect other people's schedules and fulfill commitments, he or she is not a Chaos Creator. Chaos Creators bring disorganization to a whole new level. They're so disorganized that they waste not only their own time and energy, but also that of everyone around them.

There are two defining traits all Chaos Creators share:

1. They create chaos both for others and for themselves.
2. They almost never accept responsibility for the chaos they cause.

Oh, sure, some may claim—loudly and often—that they want to be more organized. But deep down—and often aloud, too—Chaos Cre-

---

You Can't Escape Them

Whatever your job, career, or position, there's no escaping Chaos Creators—they're everywhere. You may see a reflection of yourself or your colleagues in one or more of these roles:

Captain Chaos: A basket-case boss

Chaos cadet: An overwhelmed secretary or assistant

Chaos colleagues: Harried coworkers or partners

Chaos colony: Disorganized employees or subordinates

Chaos clientele: Crazy-making clients or customers

In the chapters that follow, you'll find real-life descriptions of Chaos Creators in each of these roles, along with actual chaos-conquering strategies that were utilized successfully.

ators feel that others are to blame. One of the key reasons they keep causing chaos is that they are completely blind to the connection between their chaotic behavior and the chaos that follows them everywhere. Of course, it's always easier to point the finger of blame toward others instead of toward yourself.

The Art of Creating Chaos

Maybe you suspect you're a Chaos Creator because your extreme disorganization continually causes problems for yourself and others. Or perhaps you really aren't a Chaos Creator but in fact have been the victim of one. Either way, this much is true: No matter what your (or their) vocation, location, or level of education is, Chaos Creators always have the same effect—causing chaos and confusion for themselves and almost anyone they work with, in all types of situations.

Chaos Creators accomplish this specifically by:

- ♦ Not returning phone calls (ever, sometimes, or only eventually)
- ♦ Not answering correspondence (ever, sometimes, or only eventually)
- ♦ Being unreliable—not following through on duties or obligations
- ♦ Blowing deadlines—their own and therefore others'
- ♦ Losing paperwork (especially documents that affect others)
- ♦ Borrowing things and not returning them
- ♦ Repeatedly rescheduling dates or times of appointments
- ♦ Not showing up for scheduled appointments or meetings
- ♦ Showing up unprepared for meetings or appointments
- ♦ Running late—and making others late as a result

This structure of chaos is built on an underlying foundation that is so flawed it allows commitments, deadlines, promises, and obligations to consistently slip through the cracks . . . and onto someone's head. Perhaps yours?

Consistent Chaos Is Key

Hey, we all mess up once in a while, right? None of us is always on time. And who among us hasn't missed a deadline or a meeting? Does that make us all Chaos Creators?

In a word, no. It's true that even the most organized people suffer temporary lapses. To paraphrase a popular expression, "Chaos happens." Such bouts can be triggered by a variety of major stressors, including personal crises (such as health problems, death of a loved one, divorce) and lifestyle disruptions (e.g., a move, a new baby, downsizing).

But if people are embarrassed by their slipups, take responsibility for the chaos they cause, don't try to blame others, are willing to accept

◆◆◆

Chaos Magnets

Some people apparently have the uncanny ability to attract chaos without actually creating it themselves—or so they claim. They get a great new job only to discover that the boss who started out as Mr. Wonderful is actually a chaos-creating fiend; or their initially helpful cubicle mates have turned out to be demons of disorder. They start their own business only to be plagued by cancellation-prone clients, unreliable vendors, or dishonest employees. No matter where they go or what they do, chaos seems to follow.

Bad karma? (East Coast translation: "bad luck.") Perhaps. But more likely, the root of the problem is bad choices and/or a bad attitude. If you've become a chaos magnet, I recommend that you take a good hard look at your past choices to see if you can discern a pattern. (You may need to get some outside help for this.) As for your attitude, we'll be covering that in Chapter 8. In the meantime, for instant attitude improvement, resolve to stop telling everyone about your chaos horror stories. (Unless you're paying them to listen—or they're paying you to talk.) It's time for you to move on.

◆◆◆

help, and make sincere efforts to return to their formerly organized selves, they are not Chaos Creators.

The key here is consistency of behavior. True Chaos Creators cause chaos routinely, not rarely. What's more, they almost never hold themselves accountable for the havoc they wreak, preferring to blame their chaos on coworkers, computers, companies, their own creativity—whatever or whomever is most convenient.

How to Use This Book

Conquering Chaos at Work is not a "tips" book—it is a step-by-step strategizing manual. Although it does include a number of tips that I have found to be effective for many people, it is not a compendium of bite-sized axioms or Band-Aid–style platitudes. The book is organized into three sections:

Part I, "Classifying Chaos," features a unique self-assessment tool, the Chaos Questionnaire. Take it, and find out the truth about both your own potentially chaos-causing habits and those of virtually anyone with whom you work. You'll also discover how to identify exactly which types of chaos are consistently disrupting your work flow. Classifying chaos is a key step—you must be able to recognize the enemy in order to conquer it.

Part II, "Controlling Chaos," describes specific tactics, techniques, and tools to help you cope with the five key Chaos Categories—time, memory, communication, information, and projects.

Part III, "Conquering Chaos," takes you beyond organizing and shows you how to become a Chaos Conqueror by strategizing. It includes use-it-now forms and real-life case histories that offer both immediate and long-term solutions to help you deal with anyone who creates chaos for you at work.

Don't Be a Victim of Chaos

How you deal with your own chaos-creating tendencies and how you interact with the Chaos Creators around you will affect your steps up or down the ladder of success. Unless you know how to counteract chaos (yours and others') and cope with those who create it, you're destined to become a victim of chaos. So these are your options: You can let chaos-inducing traits derail your career, disrupt your life, and destroy your sanity. Or you can become a Chaos Conqueror and eliminate (or at least reduce) chaos—and live happily ever after. The choice is yours.

Through the years, I've learned that I can't overemphasize the importance of maintaining a sense of humor when working with Chaos Creators—but I'll try.

So choose to chuckle, inwardly if necessary, at the pitfalls and occasional pratfalls you're destined to encounter in the workplace (such as tripping over a coworker's carelessly placed briefcase and spilling coffee in his lap). And remember . . . humor empowers you to look past the problems of the present so you can obsess about the annoyances of the future.

How to Talk Like a Chaos Conqueror

Before you can walk the walk, you've got to know how to talk the talk. Here are some Chaos Conqueror terms to get you started.

Chaos Categories: Time-related, memory-related, communication-related, information-related, project-related.

Chaos Conqueror: One who consistently counteracts chaos by using the strategies described in this book.

Chaos Creator: One who consistently creates chaos.

Chaos Log: Record-keeping tool used for tracking chaos sources and frequency. (See Chapter 8.)

Chaos Trait Types:
- ♦ The **Bureaucratic Chaos Creator** (BCC) exacerbates chaos by passing the buck after wrapping it in red tape.
- ♦ The **Creative Chaos Creator** (CCC) creates chaos by losing the buck and using the red tape to make paperweights.
- ♦ The **Deceptive Chaos Creator** (DCC) camouflages chaos by hiding both the red tape and the buck in a drawer somewhere.
- ♦ The **Oblivious Chaos Creator** (OCC) doesn't notice any chaos even while sitting in the midst of piles of red tape (and denies having seen the buck as well).

Clutter-Mutter: Involuntary mantra ("Where is it? Where is it?") mumbled by victims of Treasure Hunt Syndrome. (See Chapter 4.)

Deadline Deadbeat: One who consistently misses deadlines. (See Chapter 7.)

File-o-phobe: One who consistently demonstrates a fear of filing. (See Chapter 6.)

Gap-Time: Time scheduled to accommodate foreseeable delays. (See Chapter 3.)

Mess Maven: One who is well-organized yet messy. Mess Mavens function well amidst their own clutter and apparent disorder. (See Chapters 2 and 8.)

Overwhelm: A condition that causes temporary paralysis of the decision-making muscles. (See Chapter 4.)

Paper hangover: Temporary condition caused by overexposure to paper and overstrained decision-making muscles. Symptoms include glazed eyes, impaired focus, and an inability to make rational decisions. (See Chapter 6.)

Paperosis misplacea: Highly contagious condition evidenced by the visible manifestation of information-related chaos, aka piles and piles of paper. (See Chapter 6.)

Phone-o-holic: One who continually spends excessive or unnecessary time on the telephone. (See Chapter 5.)

Phone-o-phobe: One who consistently avoids making or returning telephone calls. (See Chapter 5.)

Pile pilot: One who navigates piles of paper. (See Chapter 6.)

Redundant file syndrome (RFS):	Recurring tendency to set up duplicate, redundant, or excess files with different file names. (See Chapter 6.)
Sidetracking:	Condition caused by lack of focus. (See Chapters 3 and 6.)
SOP:	Stereotype of the Organized Person. (See Chapters 2 and 9.)
Subscribitis:	Condition caused by subscribing to more publications than can be read in a lifetime. (See Chapter 6.)
Treasure Hunt Syndrome:	Recurring tendency to hunt frantically for misplaced items. Victims of Treasure Hunt Syndrome become subconsciously dependent on the euphoric rush they experience upon finding lost things during their hunting expeditions. (See Chapters 1, 3, and 4.)
V & V:	Verbalizing and vocalizing, a memory management tactic. (See Chapter 4.)
White space:	Calendar space left deliberately unfilled to accommodate unforeseen delays and emergencies. (See Chapter 3.)

PART I

Classifying Chaos

CHAPTER 1

Are You a Chaos Creator or a Victim of One?

What You Need to Know About Chaos and Those Who Cause It

CHAPTER 2

Chaos Conquerors, Organized People, and Mess Mavens:

The Truth About Being Organized

OVERVIEW

♦ What is chaos, who causes it, and why?

♦ What does it really mean to be disorganized?

♦ What does it really mean to be organized?

♦ Is "Chaos Creator" just a new way of saying "slob"?

♦ What's the difference between an organized person and a Chaos Conqueror?

As you discover the answers to these and other questions in the two chapters that follow, you'll be exposed to a different way of thinking about the process and purpose of being organized. You'll also gain a clearer understanding of what it means to be disorganized. These insights will allow you to cope more effectively in your workplace, no matter how chaotic it is right now.

The Chaos Questionnaire in Chapter 1 will help you figure out to what degree you create chaos, which type of Chaos Creator you may be, and who or what are your prime chaos culprits. This chapter also offers insights into what chaos really is—and what it isn't. Expect to be surprised and inspired.

In Chapter 2, you'll discover why being organized doesn't necessarily mean having a perpetually tidy work space and a strictly structured routine. You'll see which traits and habits the truly organized possess, learn the key differences between organized people and Chaos Conquerors, and find out what it means to be a Mess Maven. Expect to be enlightened and motivated.

1

Are You a Chaos Creator or a Victim of One?

WHAT YOU NEED TO KNOW ABOUT CHAOS AND THOSE WHO CAUSE IT

Chaos is a name for any order that produces confusion in our minds.

—GEORGE SANTAYANA

*O*verall, Gerri was an okay boss. Bill, her overworked assistant, appreciated how good she was about sharing credit and giving praise. On the other hand, Gerri was also good at creating chaos and placing blame—usually on him.

Bill tried hard to keep things running smoothly. But the situation finally boiled over after one particularly chaotic week in which Gerri . . .

♦ Accused Bill of misplacing an important file—which he eventually located beneath a pile of papers under her desk

♦ Told several callers she hadn't received phone messages they had left, implying that Bill didn't pass the information on to her

♦ Showed up an hour late to pick up a business associate at the airport, again blaming Bill by claiming he had told her the wrong arrival time.

What Is Chaos?

When I refer to chaos, I'm not necessarily talking about clutter. Clutter isn't chaos—it's merely a visible manifestation of perceived chaos. It's possible to have chaos without clutter, and clutter without chaos, as you'll see in the coming chapters. Chaos is more complicated than just clutter.

In the workplace, chaos is created when people regularly:

◆ Circumvent systems and procedures, thereby disrupting work flow

◆ Neglect correspondence and phone messages, both their own and that of others

◆ Show up unprepared for meetings and appointments

◆ Expect others to cover for them when they let things slide

◆ Forget important details, then "delegate" blame for any resulting problems

◆ Stretch deadlines—and everyone's patience—to the breaking point

◆ Spend more time looking for things than accomplishing them

◆ Clog desks (or entire offices) with paper

◆ Disclaim responsibility for the chaos and confusion they cause

Bill was so upset he threatened to quit. Gerri finally acknowledged she had a problem, and promised to meet with Bill first thing Monday morning. Over the weekend Bill relaxed a little, feeling certain that things would get better. But his relief was short-lived. Gerri never showed up for their meeting.

Forgetful? Yes. Disorganized? Certainly. Malicious? No. Gerri was a classic Chaos Creator, and Bill was simply one of her victims.

Get a Grip—Not a Gripe

What if Gerri *had* shown up for her meeting with Bill? Would their discussion really have accomplished anything? Probably not, because Bill had no real plan in mind. Grievances galore, yes; but ideas for solutions? None.

Bill's lack of planning is typical. When it comes to conquering chaos—whether self-created or caused by others—most people tend to do at least one of two things: gripe and shop. Between complaining about chaos problems and shopping for organizing gadgets, it's easy to stay busy without actually fixing anything.

Of course, griping and/or buying stuff seems much more fun than planning an effective course of action, especially if you're unaccustomed to strategizing. So go ahead—gripe and shop to your heart's content. But when you're finally ready to stop wallowing in chaos and start moving forward, here's how to proceed.

Ready, Set . . . Focus

The first step is to accurately assess your current chaos condition. This will enable you to focus on the best strategies for solutions. The Chaos Questionnaire that follows is an assessment tool designed to help you complete this first step.

Note to clever and impatient readers: If you're the kind of person who finds questionnaires a chore and a bore, I totally empathize. For me these quiz-type things are usually frustrating time wasters—the questions often bear little relation to reality, the answer options tend to include absolutes such as "Always" and "Never" (which always never apply to *my* life, anyway), and the scoring invariably contains putdowns disguised as feeble attempts at humor (apparently intended to make you feel silly no matter how well you did). So when I created the Chaos Questionnaire, I made sure to leave out all those things that annoy me about questionnaires!

Instead, I designed it to serve two purposes:

1. As an *assessment tool*—to help you discover useful insights about yourself and the people with whom you work; and

2. As a *time-saving tool*—to show you which parts of this book to focus on first for your specific needs.

In about 10 minutes (the time it takes to complete the questionnaire), you'll not only have new insight, you'll also have an effective, customized "skimming strategy" for reading this book. Your assessment will show you specifically which chapters you need most. (Ideally, I hope you'll read every word from cover to cover; realistically, however, I know you may hop, flip, and skim around these pages. So you may as well skim strategically!)

◆◆

Habits vs. Traits

What's the difference between chaos-causing habits and traits? *Habits* are specific recurring actions or inactions; *traits* dictate the manner or style in which the habits are perpetuated. For example, Gerri has a habit of forgetting—she forgets where she puts things; she forgets what people tell her. However, like all good Chaos Creators, Gerri's natural inclination (trait) is to deny responsibility for the chaos caused by her forgetfulness. Because of her particular *chaos trait type* (one of four identifiable types that differ subtly yet significantly), the way in which she absolves herself of responsibility is to blame someone else—namely, Bill.

There's another key difference between traits and habits: traits are inborn and tend to be immutable; habits are acquired and, therefore, potentially changeable. These distinctions will be worth remembering when you are planning your future chaos-conquering strategies.

Being able to classify your own chaos-causing habits as well as those of others can help you prevent, or at least minimize, chaos. Chaos traits, however, tend to be extremely difficult to recognize in yourself; it is easier (not to mention more fun) to spot them in your coworkers. Identifying their chaos trait types will ultimately enable you to anticipate how—and even when—chaos may occur.

◆◆

How the Chaos Questionnaire Works

The questionnaire has two sections. The first section is about you: it's designed to reveal to what degree you may be causing chaos and which specific kinds of chaos-causing habits you need help with.

The second section is about the people with whom you work: its purpose is to identify specifically who is causing chaos for you, their chaos-causing habits, and their chaos trait types.

The Chaos Questionnaire will help you honestly identify three crucial chaos factors in your workplace:

- ♦ Chaos categories: What kinds do you need the most help with?

- ♦ Chaos channels: Who, specifically, is causing the most chaos?

- ♦ Chaos creators: Which types are you dealing with?

Completing the Chaos Questionnaire is your first step toward becoming a Chaos Conqueror. Here's how to get the most value from taking it.

1. Arrange to spend an uninterrupted block of time (a minimum of 10 minutes) filling in the blanks and assessing your responses.
2. Be as honest as you can. You may want to ask someone you trust for feedback on some of your responses.
3. Disregard any items that do not apply.
4. Avoid skipping ahead to the Scoring and Evaluation sections; doing so may cause you to unconsciously "cheat" by adjusting your responses.

The Chaos Questionnaire

PART I: ARE YOU CREATING CHAOS FOR YOURSELF OR OTHERS?

For each of the following queries, check either:

F (Frequently, e.g., 4–5 out of 5 times)
S (Sometimes, e.g., 2–3 out of 5 times)
R (Rarely, e.g., less than 2 out of 5 times)
Note: Leave blank any that do not apply to you.

	F	S	R
1. Do you arrive 10 minutes late or more for work, appointments, and/or meetings?			
2. Do you break or cancel appointments at the last minute?			
3. Have colleagues remarked about your lack of punctuality?			
4. Do you underestimate how much time you need to allocate for routine tasks and activities?			
5. Do you lose track of time (talking on the phone, doing paperwork, e-mailing)?			
6. Do you forget to return "borrowed" items (staplers, books, files, etc.) or fail to put them back where they belong?			
7. Do you neglect to write down dates, assignments, and tasks, either those you give yourself or those others give you?			
8. Do you have trouble completing projects because you've forgotten key details?			
9. Do you need to be reminded regularly of recurring obligations and tasks?			
10. Do you forget where you put things (keys, pager, supplies) and/or forget frequently used names, phone numbers, passwords, etc.?			
11. At day's end, do you find yourself with a pile of unreturned phone messages?			

	F	S	R
12. Do people need to call at least twice before you return their calls?			
13. Do you inadvertently neglect, or delay, answering correspondence (paper or e-mail)?			
14. Do you inadvertently neglect, or delay, sending requested or promised information?			
15. When you make requests or give assignments, do people misunderstand your instructions?			
16. Do you tend to avoid reading and/or have to reread materials in order to comprehend them?			
17. Do you misplace or lose paper and/or electronic information (notes, computer files, disks, etc.)?			
18. Is it difficult for you to accurately process information (fill out forms, write reports, input data)?			
19. Do you have trouble making decisions?			
20. Do piles of unread or unsorted paper accumulate anywhere in your work space?			
21. Do you put off planning or mapping out projects?			
22. After starting a project, do you get sidetracked (for one reason or another) before its completion?			
23. Do you miss deadlines—your own and others'?			
24. Once a project is mapped out and assigned to you, do you put off getting started?			
25. If you delegate a task that requires monitoring, do you neglect following up on its progress?			

SCORING FOR PART I

Tally your score by assigning the following numerical equivalent to each answer. *Note:* If you left any questions unanswered because they did not apply, you may need to average your score accordingly.

$$F = 5 \text{ points} \qquad S = 3 \text{ points} \qquad R = 1 \text{ point}$$

Score: _____

- ◆ If it's 75–125 . . .   You are creating chaos consistently.

- ◆ If it's 50–75 . . .   You are causing chaos intermittently.

- ◆ If it's 25–50 . . .   You do not seem to be a major source of chaos.

◆◆

Chaos Cure Shortcut

If you're in a hurry to get help, here's a shortcut. Check out the chapters relating to your specific chaos-causing habits. The questions in Part I are grouped into five key areas; if your score is high (15–25) in at least one of these areas, it is likely that you're creating chaos for yourself or others. So . . .

- ◆ A high score in questions 1–5=
  You need help with *time management*;
  see Chapter 3.
- ◆ A high score in questions 6–10=
  You need help with *memory management*;
  see Chapter 4.
- ◆ A high score in questions 11–15=
  You need help with *communication management*;
  see Chapter 5.
- ◆ A high score in questions 16–20=
  You need help with *information management*;
  see Chapter 6.
- ◆ A high score in questions 21–25=
  You need help with *project management*;
  see Chapter 7.

◆◆

The Chaos Questionnaire

PART II: IDENTIFYING AND CATEGORIZING YOUR CHAOS CREATORS

Fill in the names or initials of any people in your workplace who come to mind as you read each of the situations and accompanying completion phrases described below. Feel free to fill in the name/initials anywhere it is applicable (even in more than one lettered blank per situation). *Note:* Some of the situations may not apply; likewise, not all of the completion phrases will describe your specific experiences. Leave blank any that do not apply to you.

Example:

Here's how Bill might respond to Situation 4.

4. **When this person borrows items (files, supplies, etc.) and forgets to return them, he/she . . .**
   a. Pretends that he/she did return them, implying that someone else may be at fault or claims "I'm just too busy to have to remember things like that"

   _____

   b. Tries to laugh it off and/or apologizes

   _____

   c. Claims not to remember having borrowed them
   *Gerri*_____

   d. Attempts to replace the missing item with something else

   _____

---

1. **When this person often turns in work late, he/she tends to . . .**
   a. Justify the lateness without admitting the problem (e.g., making it sound as if other work he/she was doing was far more important, whether true or not), and/or may suggest that someone else caused the problem

   _____

    b. Find an interesting or entertaining way to distract attention from the problem, or at least has a "good" excuse

    c. Act as though he/she is not even aware there is a problem

    d. Absolve him/herself from all culpability by blaming "events beyond my control"

2. **This person rarely arrives at the scheduled time (for work, appointments, or meetings); instead he/she usually . . .**
    a. Arrives unprepared but makes a conspicuous point of being early, often ridiculing latecomers

    b. Arrives late, but has a humorous or elaborate excuse

    c. Arrives late but seems unaware of it, neither apologizing nor making excuses

    d. Arrives a few minutes early but may claim to have arrived very early, thus giving him/her an excuse to leave prematurely—for example, before work assignments are distributed

3. **I find myself having to repeatedly remind him/her . . .**
    a. To follow through on what he/she promised to do

    b. To follow important procedures

    c. About almost everything, including how to operate certain things (computer functions, coffee machine, workplace equipment)

    d. To stop using obsolete or redundant materials or proce-
dures

4. When this person borrows items (files, supplies, etc.) and forgets to return them, he/she . . .
    a. Pretends that he/she did return them, implying that some-one else may be at fault or claims "I'm just too busy to have to remember things like that"

    b. Tries to laugh it off and/or apologizes

    c. Claims not to remember having borrowed them

    d. Attempts to replace the missing item with something else

5. When I'm on the phone or having a face-to-face conversa-tion with this person, he/she . . .
    a. Makes it sound like he/she has everything under control, but neglects to give me crucial details and/or frequently misun-derstands my instructions

    b. May be fun to talk with but rarely follows through on ideas or suggestions discussed

    c. Tends to monologue: when I try to get a word in edgewise, he/she may suddenly cut the conversation short as if to imply that I talk too much

    d. Usually keeps the conversation brief, promises to get back to me—but doesn't

6. When I get memos, letters, and/or e-mail from this person, I notice . . .
   a. Correspondence from him/her tends to look good at first glance but usually lacks clarity and/or key details

   b. Correspondence from him/her may look sloppy or contain careless typos, but is often well written

   c. Correspondence from him/her completely misses the point, often containing mostly irrelevant material

   d. Correspondence from him/her usually contains redundant material (e.g., expressing the same idea in several ways)

7. This person's paperwork . . .
   a. Is kept mostly hidden away, but not in order, and is rarely processed properly

   b. Is mostly piled or spread all over his/her work space and is rarely processed properly

   c. May be filed and/or piled, but is rarely processed properly

   d. Is kept mostly in order (often in binders and/or folders) but is rarely processed properly

8. This person produces reports or other work products that . . .
   a. Appear thorough but are actually filled with inaccuracies

   b. Contain worthwhile material but are poorly organized

   c. Appear not to relate to the stated or assigned purpose

   d. Basically duplicate previous work

9. When I have to work on a project with this person, I . . .
   a. End up doing more than my share of the work because he/she neglects to complete key tasks (while continually claiming "everything's on track!")

   b. End up spending too much time helping him/her stay focused on the task at hand

   c. End up having to redo or fix much of this person's work because he/she seems to have a project in mind that's different than the one we're supposed to be working on

   d. End up frustrated by his/her ability to make things more complicated and/or time-consuming than necessary

10. When it comes to deadlines, this person . . .
   a. Gets his/her project work in on time but it's incomplete or inadequate (apparently he/she hopes no one will notice all the gaps)

   b. Apparently thinks of them as more of a starting point than a completion point, and invariably gets things done late—although the results may be worthwhile

   c. Seems oblivious to other people's but expects them to respect his/hers

   d. Has a knack for creating delays and/or getting extensions

EVALUATING YOUR RESPONSES TO PART II

Now that you've identified your Chaos Creator(s), the classifications below will help you to locate the chapters that target your specific needs. To plan your skimming strategy, print Chaos Creator name(s) or initials in the blanks that correspond to your Part II responses.

SITUATIONS	CHAOS-CAUSING HABITS	NAME(S)/INITIALS	FOR IMMEDIATE HELP
1 and 2 =	Time-related	_____	Chapter 3
3 and 4 =	Memory-related	_____	Chapter 4
5 and 6 =	Communication-related	_____	Chapter 5
7 and 8 =	Information-related	_____	Chapter 6
9 and 10 =	Project-related	_____	Chapter 7

CHAOS-CAUSING TRAITS	NAME(S)/INITIALS	FOR IMMEDIATE HELP

Name or initials that you marked next to . . .

- a's = Someone who uses deception to disguise disorganization: a *Deceptive Chaos Creator* (DCC) _____ Chapter 9
- b's = Someone who confuses chaos with creativity: a *Creative Chaos Creator* (CCC) _____ Chapter 10
- c's = Someone who is in denial about his/her own chaos-causing ways: an *Oblivious Chaos Creator* (OCC) _____ Chapter 11
- d's = Someone who uses bureaucratic methods to cultivate chaos: a *Bureaucratic Chaos Creator* (BCC) _____ Chapter 12

Example:

If Bill were to complete Part II of the questionnaire, he would discover that Gerri is an Oblivious Chaos Creator with memory-related chaos habits. He would therefore know to pay particular attention to Chapters 4 and 11 while planning his chaos-conquering strategies. *Note:* It is fairly common for Chaos Creators to have more than one category of chaos-causing habits. A mixture of traits is also common—for example, a Deceptive may have Bureaucratic traits; a Creative may share Oblivious traits.

◆◆

Another Chaos Cure Shortcut

On page 156, the Case Histories Organizational Chart provides an overview of the specific chaos categories and trait types profiled in the case histories along with page numbers, so you can go right to the ones that most closely relate to your own Chaos Creator situation.

◆◆

From Chaos to Congratulations

Now that you've completed the two-part Chaos Questionnaire, let's look at what the results reveal in more detail.

If the questionnaire indicates that you are definitely a key source of chaos in your workplace, congratulations! Your ability to identify yourself as a current Chaos Creator is an important step toward becoming a Chaos Conqueror. Why? Because it demonstrates your potential willingness to take responsibility for the chaos you cause and how it affects others. By owning up to being a Chaos Creator, you're finally becoming accountable for your actions—a definite improvement over blaming and denying. You can look forward to an improved workplace atmosphere; not only will you become more effective, but your colleagues will be overjoyed. (Eventually they may also become envious of your superior organizational skills and improved status. But let's not get carried away with these fantasies just yet.)

If the questionnaire showed that people other than yourself are the primary source of your workplace chaos, then congratulations are in order for you too. (They may be the only thing that's in order, but I guarantee that will change.) The fact that you are not actively contributing to chaotic conditions—and I'm taking your word on this—puts you squarely on the path to becoming a Chaos Conqueror. Your inborn or acquired organizing abilities will be put to the test: you'll discover how to utilize, maximize, and ultimately improve them without, it is hoped, alienating the Chaos Creators with whom you work. (Of course, they may already be alienated—or even aliens. But those issues are covered in other books.)

What Are Your Chaos Categories?

While working with hundreds of clients over the past two decades, I've had ample opportunities to analyze chaos. Naturally, I was compelled to figure out a way to categorize it. After years of unscientific research, I have come to the conclusion that most workplace chaos is rooted in at least one of five areas: time, memory, communication, information, and projects. In Chapters 3 to 7, I'll share my secrets for conquering each of these five types of chaos. But first you need to know just the basics.

Time-related chaos symptoms include regularly running late for appointments or meetings and often making others late as a result; frequently rescheduling appointments, invariably at the last minute; rarely getting work done on time.

Memory-related chaos symptoms include continually forgetting to write things down or get things done; losing materials; relying on others to resurrect missed appointments, reconstruct fragmented ideas, and repair damaged professional relationships.

Communication-related chaos symptoms include usually neglecting to return phone calls or answer correspondence in a timely fashion, if at all; lacking strong verbal communication skills (e.g., saying one thing, meaning something else, and then claiming that others misheard); talking too much, making meetings and phone calls last twice as long as necessary.

Information-related chaos symptoms include difficulty processing or locating information; spending enormous amounts of time (including other people's) looking for misplaced papers, disks, and/or electronic documents.

Project-related chaos symptoms include routinely missing project task deadlines, often causing others to miss theirs; difficulties with planning, preparation, and fol-

◆◆◆◆◆◆◆◆◆◆◆◆◆◆◆◆◆◆◆◆◆◆◆◆◆◆◆◆◆◆◆◆◆◆◆◆◆

Chaotic or Hectic?

Chaotic workplaces are not the same as hectic ones. A hectic atmosphere is one that has a sense of controlled frenzy. Hospital emergency rooms, television news rooms, and the stock exchange are examples of hectic workplaces that cannot afford to operate in a consistently chaotic manner. The opposite is true of many bureaucracies, where seemingly calm surfaces often mask yawning chasms of continual chaos.

◆◆◆◆◆◆◆◆◆◆◆◆◆◆◆◆◆◆◆◆◆◆◆◆◆◆◆◆◆◆◆◆◆◆◆◆◆

low-through. Project-related chaos combines elements of the other four chaos categories.

Which Type of Chaos Creator Are You Working With?

During my years of helping my clients conquer chaos, I began to notice certain patterns in the way many people create chaos. Although individuals may create chaos for different reasons, there are specific personality traits that seem to show up again and again in true Chaos Creators. I've identified four main Chaos Creator trait types (Chaos Creators can also be a *combination* of these trait types).

1. *Deceptive Chaos Creators (DCCs).* DCCs often disguise their disorganization by creating the illusion that they have everything under control. They may be perfectionists who have difficulty prioritizing, perhaps spending more time tidying their desks than accomplishing any real work. They have a knack for implying that others are to blame for any resulting chaos. (See Chapter 9.)
2. *Creative Chaos Creators (CCCs).* CCCs surround themselves with clutter and may even appear to revel in disarray. When they foul up, they blame the chaos on their own "creativity" and blithely expect others to pick up all the balls they drop. (See Chapter 10.)
3. *Oblivious Chaos Creators (OCCs).* OCCs are in complete denial about their chaos-creating tendencies. Like CCCs, they may surround themselves with visual chaos, but like DCCs they invariably blame others when everything falls apart. (See Chapter 11.)
4. *Bureaucratic Chaos Creators (BCCs).* BCCs have the perfect excuse for causing chaos, blaming whatever goes wrong on existing workplace conditions: "That's just the way it is around here." They create chaos by using the three *r*'s: rules, redundancy, and red tape. They may be efficient without being effective. (See Chapter 12.)

No matter which type of Chaos Creator you work with, you'll find effective coping strategies in Chapters 9 to 12 that can be applied to your particular situation.

◆◆◆

Chaos Creators in a Nutshell

DCCs: Know they create chaos, won't admit it, blame others

CCCs: Know they create chaos, admit it, blame creativity

OCCs: Don't know they create chaos, blame others

BCCs: May or may not know they create chaos, blame workplace

◆◆◆

Why, Oh Why?

Working amidst constant chaos can leave you feeling frustrated and fed up. On top of that, if you feel sure that you are not causing any chaos yourself, paranoia may strike: you'll start thinking that others are creating chaos on purpose, just to make your life miserable. And occasionally you may be right. (I once saw this bumper sticker, "Just because you're paranoid doesn't mean everyone isn't out to get you.") More often, though, those who create chaos are just overwhelmed, organizationally challenged beings who have gotten in over their heads. Mired in a quicksand of chaos, their struggles cause them to sink deeper; when others lend them a helping hand (voluntarily or not), Chaos Creators can drag such well-meaning rescuers down with them.

Although you or others may not deliberately cause chaos, it's possible that some Chaos Creators may have learned how to benefit from their disorganized ways. Perhaps these individuals begin to develop their manipulation muscles in childhood, then become adept at getting others to help them out with the messes they make or get into. Over time, they evolve into superior manipulators, whether consciously or unconsciously.

I've noticed that certain Chaos Creators manage to vary their exertions based on how much they use (and often abuse) the time and energy of other people. In general, Chaos Creators do not show much consideration for others or even for themselves. After all, creating chaos doesn't leave much time for being considerate.

◆◆◆

The Cost of Chaos

Chaos Creators aren't just inefficient and exasperating (which they certainly are). They're also costly to themselves, to their victims, and to their firms or organizations because of the time and materials they continually waste. In business, time really is money, so Chaos Creators technically waste both. For example:

◆ An article in *The Wall Street Journal* reported that the average U.S. executive wastes six weeks per year searching for missing information in disorganized files and desktop piles.

◆ According to the Harper's Index, the amount of time that the average American spends looking for misplaced things over the course of a lifetime is one year.

◆◆◆

Popular Excuses

In many cases, Chaos Creators simply have no idea why their actions produce chaos. Worse, they apparently don't care about the effect their chaotic habits have on others.

Of course, a plethora of popular excuses for disorganized behavior has sprung up over the past decade: Attention Deficit Disorder, Obsessive-Compulsive Disorder, Packrat Syndrome, Information Anxiety, and at least 40 different kinds of dyslexia. Some disorganized people-cum-Chaos Creators actually do have one or more of these conditions; and, in fact, there are various therapeutic options now available for them (not including the somewhat primitive "whack-over-the-head" therapy). But in my opinion, most self-diagnosed sufferers are just deluding themselves and others by providing an ailment as an alibi. The real reasons behind their disorganization are usually much less trendy.

Realistic Reasons Why People Cause Chaos

They lack training and experience. No one has ever shown them how to be any different. They haven't a clue how to set up systems and procedures to make things work smoothly.

They're organizationally impaired. They've been unable to learn basic organizing skills and may actually be incapable of maintaining order in their lives.

They're overwhelmed. They have much more to do than they can possibly handle. They need help but won't ask for it.

It's a good way to avoid work. They've learned that chaos is a good method for wriggling out of doing any real work. By getting others to pick up the slack for them, they can also pass the blame when things don't get done.

They get an adrenaline rush from all the stress. Waiting until the last minute before beginning or completing tasks, for example, can provide excitement in the form of urgency.

For some, the act of searching for misplaced things, especially while in a hurry, can provide excitement and a kind of perverse pleasure. I call this Treasure Hunt Syndrome. It appears that certain Chaos Creators subconsciously feel like explorers searching for buried treasure in the wilds of the office. When the lost object is located, the accompanying sense of relief gives them a euphoric rush. Thus these Chaos Creators may resist getting organized because they don't really want to miss out on the thrill of the hunt and the joy of discovery—and they don't seem to care that their disruptive game isn't fun for others.

When Chaos Creators are unable to find what they're looking for, however, their excitement usually turns to

---

A Crash Course in Chaos Creator Terminology

Misplaced: Item is eventually located after a frantic search.

Mislocated: Someone else put it away where it actually belongs.

Missing: "Someone else must have taken it!"

Lost: Chaos Creator has finally given up looking for it.

TREASURE HUNT SYNDROME

frustration. Once the treasure hunt has clearly become an exercise in futility, they may experience a sense of dejection. Grudgingly, they'll concede that what was "misplaced" could be redefined as "lost."

Of course, Chaos Creators often lose things. Some losses are tangible and temporary: documents, money, business cards, phone messages, calendars, day planners, keys, glasses, stamps, and other objects are found eventually—usually after Chaos Creators have disrupted busy schedules.

But ultimately, Chaos Creators lose more than just tangible objects. And much of what they lose is irreplaceable.

Examples of Lost Intangibles

PERSONAL	PROFESSIONAL	FINANCIAL
Temper	Respect	Bonuses
Time	Reputations	Raises
Energy	Relationships	Promotions

In addition to losing credibility, Chaos Creators lose both their own patience and other people's. Talk about being a loser!

But don't despair—as long as you don't lose hope or your sense of humor, help is available.

This chapter has given you the tools to uncover some important truths about yourself and your chaos. You now have the power to determine (1) whether you're a Chaos Creator or if other people really are responsible for the chaos you're battling, (2) which kind of Chaos Creator you are or you work with, and (3) the specific type(s) of chaos you need to

General Rules for Creating Chaos Efficiently

If you're going to create chaos, you may as well do it right. Here's how.

◆ Be inflexible—or too flexible.

◆ Refuse to be resourceful.

◆ Communicate unclearly.

◆ Avoid focusing.

◆ Do not follow through or keep your promises.

◆ Always expect others to follow through and keep their promises.

◆ Always expect things to be done your way.

◆ Always assume others will pick up the slack.

◆ Always expect others to be more organized than you.

◆ Change your mind often, but don't tell others unless it doesn't affect them.

conquer. You have also gained some helpful insights into why people cause chaos.

Okay, so now you have all this knowledge and power. Does this mean that you have what it takes to be a Chaos Conqueror?

Let's find out.

2

Chaos Conquerors, Organized People, and Mess Mavens:

THE TRUTH ABOUT BEING ORGANIZED

*Even if you're on the right track,
you'll get run over if you just sit there.*

—WILL ROGERS

What exactly is a Chaos Conqueror? And do you have to be organized in order to become one? Good questions.

A Chaos Conqueror is a person who consistently counteracts chaos. Being organized isn't enough to make you a Chaos Conqueror—although it's a good start. There are actually several subtle yet crucial differences between being organized and being a Chaos Conqueror.

People who are simply organized tend to use their organizing skills to get by; Chaos Conquerors use their organizing skills to get ahead. The ordinary organized person finds chaos distracting and disturbing and tries to avoid it. But chaos intrigues the Chaos Conqueror, who views it

ORGANIZED PERSON	CHAOS CONQUEROR
Perceives chaos as a problem	Views chaos as a challenge
Finds ways to avoid chaos	Seeks ways to conquer chaos
Passively maintains order	Actively counteracts chaos

as a challenge instead of a crisis and seeks ways to conquer it. *Chaos Conquerors use chaos as an opportunity to effect change.*

To become a Chaos Conqueror—or even to become less of a Chaos Creator—you may first need to become better organized. That's what the chapters in Part II will help you do.

First, however, it's important for you to get clear about what it actually means to be organized. Understanding it is essential to becoming it. But we're going to have to do a bit of digging to get to the solid gold essence of being organized. There are an awful lot of harmful half-truths, misconceptions, and mixed messages floating around out there and creating chaos.

◆◆◆◆◆◆◆◆◆◆◆◆◆◆◆◆◆◆◆◆◆◆◆◆◆◆◆◆◆◆◆◆◆◆◆◆◆

The Hurdle Jumper

Here is a way to visualize yourself as a Chaos Conqueror:

◆ You are a professional hurdle jumper.

◆ You understand and accept that hurdles will be placed along your path in a consistently inconsistent manner.

◆ You may not know exactly when or where you will encounter hurdles, but you are always prepared to encounter them.

◆ You have trained yourself to focus bifocally.

◆ You scan ahead for hurdles while keeping your eye on the finish line.

◆◆◆◆◆◆◆◆◆◆◆◆◆◆◆◆◆◆◆◆◆◆◆◆◆◆◆◆◆◆◆◆◆◆◆◆◆

Let's examine some now. I'll use them to illustrate what being organized isn't, which will then make it easier for you to understand what it is.

Mixed Messages and Stereotypes

Our society seems to have a love-hate relationship with the idea of being organized. On the one hand, it's a state many individuals and businesses supposedly aspire to. A *USA Today* survey showed that American women ranked "getting organized" as a top priority, second only to "losing weight."

On the other hand, there's a widespread, but unfounded, belief that being organized leaves no room for creativity, humor, and the fun that makes life worth living. This misconception can be traced to the myth-makers of Hollywood and Madison Avenue, who have long promoted the Stereotype of the Organized Person (SOP): unoriginal, overbearing, obsessively orderly—and ultimately joyless. Someone like Felix Unger of *The Odd Couple,* for example. Not laughing, but laughed at. Usually the "organized guy" is portrayed as either the straight man (comedically speaking) or gay. And the organized woman is still characterized as prissy, fussy, and prudish.

It doesn't help that "creativity" has become a euphemism for disorga-nization. Many Chaos Creators try to excuse their chaos by claiming, "I'm too creative to be organized." I don't buy it. The fact is, the most successful creative people are either idiosyncratically organized them-selves or are wise enough to hire organized people to help them.

When Anal Is Banal

Organized is used synonymously for everything from just plain "tidy" all the way to "anal retentive." The latter, incidentally, is a psychological term that is often employed—incorrectly—to pejoratively describe any-one who prefers order to chaos. In recent years it has become a popular putdown (neatly abbreviated to "anal") that certain Chaos Creators like to use in an apparent attempt to make organized people feel ashamed of themselves. And it's worked! I've heard many people actually apologize for being organized, and even hasten to label themselves as "anal" be-fore anyone else can do it. (Chaos Conquerors, however, do not fall into this trendy trap; they see no reason to apologize for their organizing skills. And neither should you.)

Organizing Envy

Many organized people actually shy away from the label of "organized person" and, like others, are quick to claim that they, too, "need to get more organized." Who can blame them for wanting to disassociate themselves from the anal SOP?

Think about it. Depending upon the inflection used, describing someone as "organized" may reflect admiration or admonishment; it can imply a compliment, a complaint—or both. (Envy, after all, may have many masks.)

What can you say when someone tells you, "You're so organized you make me sick"? ("Why, thank you! And here's an air-sickness bag I just happen to have on hand so you won't splatter my suit!"). Mark Twain may have said it best: "Few things are harder to put up with than the annoyance of a good example."

Neat Does Not Equal Organized

Let's assume you keep a clear desk, a briefcase with room to spare, perpetually empty in-out baskets, a clutter-free credenza. Sounds like you're an organized person, yes?

Not so fast. This description tells me only that you're a *neat* person. (Neat as in "tidy," not necessarily as in "nifty." Although for all I know, you're both.) The fact is, neat does not mean organized, and vice versa. Neatness may be a by-product of organization, but it doesn't have to be. Neatness is neatness, period. Now, don't get me wrong—I happen to like neatness. But I also recognize that it isn't an indication of effectiveness—or of anything else, for that matter.

As I tell my clients, "It's not how it looks—it's how it works, and how it helps you work, that's most important." Neatness is about form; organization is about function. After all, what's the point of having a tidy desk if you never get around to returning phone calls or answering your correspondence? Who cares how neat your office looks if you don't get your work done on time?

Obviously, neatness is desirable in many workplace situations. Especially in our Western culture, neatness is

Mess for Success?

Although I'm not advocating messy desks, I think this statistic from *The Wall Street Journal* should help dissuade those who think a neat desk is essential to success:

A 1996 poll of some 1,100 Fortune 1000 executives found that the stock value of companies whose executives had sloppy desks rose 3.5 percent the previous year, compared with a 1 percent drop for companies whose executives kept tidy desks.

often seen—rightly or wrongly—as a reflection of an individual's or company's competence and professionalism. I suppose that's why some companies even have a clean-desk policy (a rather feeble idea, in my opinion).

Of course, the importance of having tidy work habits is relative, depending on the kind of industry you work in. A surgeon with a messy office may inspire concern instead of confidence. On the other hand, an illustrator can often get away with a disorderly desk because clients view it as a sign of creativity. So depending on the type of work you do, having tidy work habits may or may not be considered important.

Since I'm called in to help people get organized, I've learned to be on guard when I walk into a new client's office or home and it looks very, very neat. What this often means is that all the drawers, cabinets, cupboards, closets, and credenzas are packed solid with paper and other clutter. In fact, some of my most disorganized Chaos Creator clients have had the tidiest-looking places.

Again, this doesn't mean that neatness and organization are mutually exclusive; far from it. But it's important to recognize that they are not synonymous, either, contrary to what you might have heard. I'm sure there are plenty of people out there (besides me, of course) who are organized and tidy, too. It's just that I don't usually get to meet them in my line of work.

As an organizing consultant, I find that I must constantly educate people about what I call the Neatness Myth. Understand this: It's much easier to neaten things up than it is to organize them so you can easily find what you're looking for.

You can quickly straighten up a disorganized pile of paper: it will become a disorganized *stack* of paper. You can hastily clear off a disastrous desk by stuffing everything on it into drawers: it might look tidy on the outside, but inside it remains a disaster. You can rapidly clean out a cluttered cabinet by cramming its contents into crates or boxes: it looks nicer, but it ain't organized!

P.S. Even tidy people (whether organized or disorganized) aren't *always* neat. The only people I know of who are able to keep everything neat every minute are the ones who live in television sitcoms or on the pages of magazines.

Mess Mavens

What if you meet many of the criteria for an organized person, but you just can't seem to keep your work area looking neat and tidy? Don't despair. Perhaps you are truly organized, but like many people you've been fooled into assuming that all messy people are disorganized. Not so. Over the years, I've encountered quite a few individuals who are untidy yet well-organized wonders. I call these amazing people Mess Mavens.

Mess Mavens function incredibly well in the midst of mountains of paper and other clutter. Sometimes they're the hardworking office heroes who manage to juggle multiple priorities for themselves and others without dropping an appointment or missing a deadline, despite their

THE MESS MAVEN

appearance of disorder and disarray. They put up with a lot of teasing about their messy tendencies, yet they respect the time, space, and workload of others.

One of my clients—I'll call her Lucy—is a perfect example of Mess Mavenhood. Lucy was an office manager whose chronically cluttered desk made her the butt of many jokes around the office. Ironically, the people who criticized Lucy the most were actually the Chaos Creators responsible for much of the mess that landed on her desk.

She kept the office running smoothly but received ridicule instead of raises because her organizational skills were masked by mess. Since she didn't "look organized" (a euphemism for "neat"), she had trouble earning the respect—and rewards—she deserved.

But Lucy recognized the real problem. "I'm so busy cleaning up other people's messes, I never have time to take care of my own!"

In some cases, however, this could be an excuse. Unlike tidy people, who find disarray distracting, many Mess Mavens are subconsciously stimulated by mess; bare surfaces make them uneasy, and get filled up quickly anyway. As long as Mess Mavens really know where everything is, they figure, "What difference does it make how it looks?" Since they're more comfortable with clutter, they often see no reason to tidy up, preferring instead to use their time to accomplish other things. (NOTE: In Chapter 8, you'll discover the steps Lucy took to become a Chaos Conqueror.)

If you're not a Mess Maven yourself but you work with people like Lucy, don't pick on them or try to change them, unless you're willing and able to tactfully offer help. As long as that person is able to accomplish everything he or she has been assigned to do, on time and without impeding your progress, then it's simply a matter of aesthetics. Personally, I'd rather work with a Mess Maven than with a Deceptive Chaos Creator who spends more time neatening than getting things done.

Organizing Is Not Cleaning

Neither organizing nor neatening have much to do with cleaning, yet many people tend to use all three terms interchangeably. If you doubt it, here's a surefire way to prove it: The next time you hear someone sigh, "I need to clean my desk," hand them a can of cleanser and a

scrubber. If they seem puzzled instead of grateful,
you'll know what they really
meant to say was either "I
need to organize my desk" or
"I need to tidy up my desk."

The cleaning/neatening/
organizing issue is, admit-
tedly, a sore point with me. I
get a bit tired of explaining
to people that as an organizer, the work I do is a lot
closer to that of a systems an-
alyst than a housecleaner.
And no, it's not the same as
"cleaning up before the maid
comes" (which is, by the way,
a good idea since it's easier to
clean bare surfaces than cluttered ones).

> ### *Terms of Confusion*
>
> *Organizing:* Putting things in a logical order for the purpose of making it easy to locate them
>
> *Decluttering:* Discarding, removing, or markedly reducing any accumulation of materials
>
> *Neatening:* Straightening, tidying, cleaning up, and/or hiding things away to create the appearance of orderliness
>
> *Cleaning:* Removing dirt via washing, vacuuming, dusting, scrubbing, and any other cleansing processes

So here's how I explain it: *Neatening* is what you do before the
cleaner comes. *Cleaning* is what the cleaner does. And *organizing* is
what you decide to do after the cleaner leaves and you are going crazy
trying to find what you hid away while you were neatening.

Organized—or Not?

Although you might not brag about it (or even if you do), perhaps you
consider yourself to be fairly well organized at work because:

- ◆ You live by the motto, "A place for everything and everything in its place," always putting things back where they belong.

- ◆ You use a time management system to plan and schedule your commitments and to-dos.

- ◆ You invariably straighten up your desk at the end of the day.

- ◆ You're usually on time for appointments and meetings.

- ◆ You don't let piles of paper develop either on or in your desk and surrounding areas.

- ◆ You rarely have to spend time looking for misplaced things—unless it's something someone else misplaced.

If the above list describes your regular work habits, you're entitled to feel a warm glow of accomplishment. (Try not to let it surface as a smug smile, though.) If that list doesn't describe you, however, don't despair. While it's true these are all valid examples of organized behavior, to me they reflect only the superficial aspects of how some, but not all, organized people function. A person could do all those things yet still manage to create chaos.

Consider It Considerate

My overall definition of being organized has more to do with the essence of what it means to be an organized person. To me, being organized is really about showing consideration for others: demonstrating trustworthiness, fulfilling obligations, keeping commitments, being reliable. Therefore, I feel that an organized person is someone who consistently chooses to behave in a considerate manner.

By considerate I don't necessarily mean courteous, although courteous and even gracious behavior can be a by-product of consideration. To me, being considerate means that you habitually consider the consequences of your actions and plan accordingly for assorted outcomes. ("Hope for the best but plan for the worst," as the saying goes.)

For instance, an organized (considerate) person knows when to say no, although doing so may appear ungracious or discourteous at times, especially to the person who's just been turned down. But ultimately, it may be the most considerate action for everyone involved. (Knowing *how* to say no graciously is a different topic entirely—one perhaps best left to Miss Manners.) Think of all the chaos that could be avoided if more people were considerate enough to say no instead of committing themselves to obligations that they do not have the time, energy, interest, ability, or resources to follow through on. But unless you are organized enough to know your limits, it's difficult to know when to say no.

Being organized does not automatically make you a considerate person—it just makes it easier for you to be one.

Organizing Is Ongoing

Being organized isn't about operating in a vacuum (or even operating a vacuum, for that matter; cleanliness and organization are different things entirely, as you now know). Unless you're in some isolated line of work (professional beachcomber, perhaps?), the degree to which you are organized is usually reflected in your dealings with other people. Again, that's why being organized is ultimately about being considerate. And the process of being organized is actually what helps you to be that way.

Organization is ongoing and never-ending. Organized people continuously invest time and effort in the process to ensure that they rarely disappoint others—or themselves. (People often say to me things like, "You're so organized. It must be easy for you to _____." [Fill in complicated, time-consuming project, such as "write a book."] To which I respond, in a gracious, considerate tone, "No, it's not easy. But being organized does make it easier." Then I try hard not to slap them.)

So, if you consistently, not intermittently, honor most of your commitments and show consideration for others, you're probably organized enough to become a Chaos Conqueror. But if you're not yet organized enough to become one, it's time you did some deep soul-searching. Because you probably *do* have what it takes to transform yourself into a Chaos Conqueror—that is, if you really want to.

Why Bother?

If you think being organized sounds like a lot of work, you're right. So, why bother to be an organized person in a chaotic world? Well, I'm not going to drone on about the benefits of being organized, saving time and money, blah blah blah. You already know all that. Thousands of magazine articles and hundreds of books have described, in endless detail, all the enviable attributes and advantages of being an organized person.

The real question is this: What would compel anyone to consistently use all that time and effort to do what it takes to be organized?

And the answer is this: Because for some people, being organized is important. So if you say you want to be more organized, but you have

◆◆◆◆◆◆◆◆◆◆◆◆◆◆◆◆◆◆◆◆◆◆◆◆◆◆◆◆◆◆◆◆◆◆◆

Too Organized?

"You can never be too rich or too thin" is a saying that needs updating, I think, now that we know the dangers of various eating disorders. I propose we change it to, "You can never be too rich or too organized." After all, it's unlikely anyone ever died from being too organized.

◆◆◆◆◆◆◆◆◆◆◆◆◆◆◆◆◆◆◆◆◆◆◆◆◆◆◆◆◆◆◆◆◆◆◆

not been willing to do what it takes to get and stay organized, then being organized may not be sufficiently important to you. Or, to put it another way, the chaos you are creating or experiencing may not cause you enough discomfort to force you to change the way you operate. (And if your behavior creates chaos for others and you do nothing to change that, the fact that you are being inconsiderate apparently doesn't bother you too much. Not that there's anything wrong with that, Attila.)

Ultimately, being organized is like anything else that takes sustained time and effort, such as staying in shape, being well-groomed, or maintaining a hobby. If you believe the results are worth the effort, you'll do whatever needs to be done to get those results. It's that simple. (Not easy, just simple.)

So, you've learned what it means to be a Chaos Conqueror. You've also discovered the truth about being organized, how to recognize and respect a Mess Maven, and why you should never, ever use the term anal retentive when referring to organized people (especially if I am within earshot).

Now it's time to begin your first lesson in conquering chaos.

Don't be late.

PART II

Controlling Chaos

OVERVIEW

Chapters 3 through 7 contain descriptions of chaos-conquering processes, procedures, and products that can help you control chaos from each of the Chaos Categories: time, memory, communication, information, and projects. As you journey through these chapters, you'll see how these five types of chaos are interconnected—as are the corresponding chaos cures.

Since I didn't want to overwhelm you with too many options, I've included only my favorite, most effective methods for preventing and managing chaos. Expect to be edified and intrigued.

Here are some points to keep in mind while you evaluate the chaos-conquering options in the chapters ahead.

♦ **DO** think about the economics of conquering chaos before spending money or time. Your position and situation will dictate whether or not various expenditures are reimbursable. It's wise to do your homework in advance and figure out some type of budget before investing anything in the process.

♦ **DON'T** fall into the trap of buying temptingly trendy organizing trinkets just because they "look organized." You might end up contributing clutter instead of counteracting chaos. It's unlikely that stuff like chrome-trimmed Lucite desk accessories and hand-painted china pencil holders will do anything more than create a fleeting frisson of order. Better to save your money and put it toward what surely will be a much-needed vacation.

♦ **DON'T** presume that if something works well for you, it must work as well for everyone (a common misconception of many well-meaning people). This narrow-minded presumption causes you to unconsciously restrict your options, thereby limiting your chaos-conquering abilities. A side effect: You'll radiate a subtle but perceptible know-it-all aura that can alienate the very people you're trying to help.

♦ **DO** make a point of carefully observing your own and others' chaos-creating habits for several weeks. This doesn't mean you have to hire a detective or go peeking through keyholes. Instead, make a conscious effort to notice if there's any pattern or consistency of style in the way you and your coworkers operate. For example, does incoming mail always get piled on a particular corner of a desk or credenza? That specific spot could be the ideal place to locate a paper-flow system (see page 137). Are appointments often forgotten and calendars or planners continually misplaced? A time management software system with bells-and-whistles sound effects may be the answer. The point is, your observations should help dictate the best course of action.

❖ ❖ ❖ ❖ ❖ *Watch-Out Windows* ❖ ❖ ❖ ❖ ❖

Throughout the next five chapters, you'll find Watch-Out Windows like this one. Their purpose is to . . .

♦ Remind you to periodically step back and take a look at your own and other people's patterns and peculiarities from a different vantage point. Watch-Out Windows give you a framework to look through.

♦ Alert you to the tactics you or your Chaos Creators use, consciously and unconsciously. If you don't watch out, it's easy to get caught in mind traps.

♦ Pinpoint for you my most successful strategies for counteracting chaos.

Watch-Out Windows capture the essence of my in-the-trenches experiences—over a decade's worth of observing and training hundreds of Chaos Creators in their natural habitats. (What an image!)

3

Tackling
Time-Related Chaos

I've been on a calendar but never on time.
—MARILYN MONROE

One of my favorite time management books, *How to Live on 24 Hours a Day* by Arnold Bennett, is packed with timely tips and timeless ideas. But don't bother looking for it at a bookstore, whether on-site or on-line; it's out of print. It was published in 1910.

My point is this: Time management is not a new science—although many people today seem to think it is. Do you really suppose there was more time in the past, back in the good old days before phones and computers and fax machines descended upon us and ate up our time by making everything go too fast?

Managing time has always been a puzzle for humans. But nowadays, plenty of us seem to be having particular difficulty with it. And why not? After all, it's not as though time management is taught in school. Some people figure it out for themselves—often with the aid of books, audio-tapes, videotapes, seminars, or consultants—but many others never do. And a certain percentage of those who don't, become Chaos Creators.

Two Types of Time

Time management and organization go together like cookies and milk (or chaos and confusion). Planning your time takes organization, and organization takes time—specifically, two types of time. The first is what I call Project Time. That's the time you spend working on projects—setting up systems (e.g., databases, accounting programs, filing systems), creating and developing new products or materials, clearing out existing accumulations of clutter. Project Time gets all the glory.

The second type of time is Maintenance Time. This type of time tends to be undervalued and under-appreciated. I have a saying: "Life is 5 percent joy, 5 percent grief, and 90 percent maintenance." Think about it: Virtually 90 percent of what we do in life is stuff we have to keep doing over and over and over again—answering calls and correspondence, filing, invoicing and bill paying, inputting data . . .

No matter who you are or at what level you work, adequate Maintenance Time is necessary for chaos prevention. Even Michael Eisner, CEO and chairman of The Walt Disney Co. and one of the highest-paid executives in the world, claims in his autobiography, *Work in Progress,* to spend 75 percent of his time on maintenance tasks such as returning calls, answering his mail, keeping his desk clear, and putting out "each day's small fires before they spread." Otherwise, he writes, "there is no way I can comfortably focus the rest of my attention on what matters most—namely, trying to add value to the creative process."

Maintenance Time is a concept that people in general and Chaos Creators in particular have trouble with. There's this misperception that once they've cleared off a desk or cleaned out a file drawer, it should magically stay that way. Of course it won't, any more than a garden will stay weeded or dishes will stay washed; yet people keep hoping that next time, maybe it will. (But ask them if they believe in elves and fairies, and they'll laugh in your face.)

Neglecting Maintenance Time actually creates the need for more Project Time, because when something isn't maintained it may eventually cease to function and/or become an unsightly mess. Then it needs to be overhauled, reorganized, repaired, or replaced, any one of which constitutes a project and often a headache as well.

Understanding and accepting the Maintenance Time equation isn't easy, but it's one of the best things you can do to put yourself or another Chaos Creator on the path to organization. How do you go about it? I recommend a four-step process.

1. Figure out approximately how much time you currently spend for each type of maintenance task relating to your job. Use the Maintenance Time Worksheet which follows to help you do this.

Maintenance Time Worksheet

Life is 5 percent joy, 5 percent grief, and 90 percent maintenance

Instructions

1. Pencil in your estimates of how much time you currently spend for each type of applicable maintenance task listed. (Some may not apply.)
2. Review your time estimates, and ask yourself whether the time you spend on maintenance is sufficient.
3. Using a different color pen or pencil, go back through the worksheet and mark in how much additional time you think should be spent, realistically, on each task.

| | ESTIMATED OR ALLOTTED TIME | |
TYPE OF MAINTENANCE	PER DAY	PER WEEK
Phone calls		
Answering	_____	_____
Returning (including "phone tag")	_____	_____
Initiating	_____	_____
Computer work		
Deleting old files	_____	_____
Backing up hard drive	_____	_____
Other: _____	_____	_____
Correspondence (including e-mail and faxes)		
Reading	_____	_____
Responding	_____	_____
Initiating	_____	_____
File work		
Filing	_____	_____
Weeding	_____	_____
Shredding	_____	_____
General maintenance		
Bookkeeping (invoicing, etc.)	_____	_____
Clutter control (putting away)	_____	_____
Mail processing	_____	_____
Preparation and follow-up	_____	_____
Reading (publications, etc.)	_____	_____
Replenishing supplies	_____	_____
Total maintenance time	_____	_____

2. After completing the worksheet, ask yourself whether the time you spend on maintenance is sufficient. Consider whether there's any connection between lack of time spent on certain tasks and any incidences of chaos. For example, let's say you're spending zero time each week on filing, and misplaced documents are a regular source of frustration. Could there possibly be a connection?
3. Using a different color pen or pencil, go back through the worksheet and mark in how much time you think should be spent, realistically, on each maintenance task so that ongoing organized results can be achieved. If, for example, you've been spending zero time on filing, figure on a *minimum* of 1 hour a week for filing maintenance.
4. Schedule that maintenance time regularly—actually mark it into your time management system calendar or whatever you use to keep track of your appointments. Keeping appointments with yourself is just as important as keeping appointments with others. So remember, no last-minute cancellations!

If you have any chaos issues (not just time-related ones), it's especially important that you take a few minutes to evaluate your completed worksheet either by yourself or with the help of a trustworthy colleague.

If, however, you believe that it's actually your coworkers who have trouble with time, the process is a bit different. Depending on your situation, it may or may not be possible to get other people to participate in filling out the worksheet. If you set a good example and lead the way (be sure to make several photocopies of the worksheet beforehand), they just might do it. Theoretically, they may then be willing to let you help evaluate their results. (Realistically, they may then be willing to beat you to a pulp. But let's hope for a kinder, gentler reception.)

If you think your coworkers' worksheet responses are, shall we say, not entirely reality-based, remember to be diplomatic about your observations. Ask whether they think the time they spend on maintenance is sufficient. Don't point out the obvious. Try to steer them toward seeing the link between lack of time allotted and chaos created. Keep in mind that guiding people toward solutions is often more effective than pushing solutions onto them.

Once the Maintenance Time deficits (whether your own or your colleagues') have been pinpointed, the next step is to figure out how to regularly and effectively schedule sufficient Maintenance Time. A good time management system is crucial to this process.

The Truth About
Time Management Systems

There are dozens of paper-based (notebook- or binder-style) time management systems on the market, ranging from the basic Week-at-a-Glance to the dependable Day-Timer to the sleek, sophisticated Franklin. They come in many sizes, colors, styles, and materials and can include any number of forms, checklists, and accessories. These systems run the gamut from strikingly simple to confusingly complex. (That's no exaggeration: some even require a workshop to explain how to use them!) Then there are all those time management software programs—it seems like a new one is being hawked every day. Not to mention handheld electronic organizers. Whew!

How do you decide which type of time management system to choose? Ironically, it takes time. There's no getting around it—finding one that works for you is a trial-and-error process. The fact is, all time management systems have this in common: They don't work for everyone. So experimenting with different options is really your best bet. Fortunately, many of them have money-back guarantees. (*Note:* A book called *Organized to Be the Best!* by Susan Silver has a detailed overview of the best time management products. See Appendix A.)

But no matter which type(s) of planner you or your chaos-causing colleagues may choose, use, and sometimes lose (as the case may be), I'll bet this much is true: It's unlikely that the system's features are being utilized effectively. And depending on your situation, there may or may not be a whole lot you're able (or willing) to do about it.

Fortunately, you don't necessarily need to do a whole lot to get positive results. Think quality, not quantity: One time management trick that works is worth dozens that don't.

The following options will give you specific ideas on how to help yourself and other tardy-making Chaos Creators become more punctual performers.

The Gap-Time Trick

One of the most common causes—and symptoms—of time-related chaos is running late. (Then again, for some folks, running late is the only exercise they get. Unless you count jumping to conclusions and stretching the truth.) Running late yourself is one thing; causing others to run late is another. And repeatedly doing so is what differentiates a true Chaos Creator from a merely dispunctual person.

Perhaps you have tried—and abandoned—various tools and methods in a fruitless attempt to stop running late yourself or to help someone else be more punctual. For example, setting timepieces ahead (anywhere from 10 minutes to an hour) sometimes works initially, but the effectiveness of this trick tends to wane. Likewise, giving artificial appointment times or deadlines can provide temporary relief, like aspirin. But before long, the chaos-causing behavior creeps back.

Gap-Time to the rescue.

Gap-Time is the term I use for the time that should be padded, like bubble-wrap, around appointments and meetings. It prevents potential schedule breakage, cracking (of jokes at your expense), and overall damage (to your professional reputation).

This is how Gap-Time works. Let's say a 12:00 lunch appointment is scheduled and it's expected to last an hour; Gap-Time might be blocked out (actually marked in the calendar) for 11:15–12:00 and 1:00–1:45. That's the approximate time needed to get to and from the appointment in a timely fashion. So, instead of just marking in "12:00 lunch," you'd put "11:15 leave; 12:00 lunch; 1:45 return." What you're doing is padding your appointment time to allow for all the things that typically might make you run late. The key truth here is this: Setting aside time to get going—and to get back—is just as important as scheduling time to get things done.

Examples of Typical Gap-Time Activities

Bathroom breaks

Chatting (on phone or in person)

Coffee breaks

Greetings and good-byes

"Treasure hunting" (looking for misplaced keys, glasses, paperwork, etc.)

Water-cooler visits

Travel (to and from appointments)

Gap-Time encompasses everything from travel time to meeting preparation time to hello-and-good-bye time. Depending on the nature of the particular appointment or meeting and the nature of the person involved, more or less time would need to be scheduled.

Without scheduled Gap-Time, certain people won't leave sufficient time before, between, and after appointments not only to get places on time but for any necessary planning and follow-up. By not visually marking, on the calendar, the blocks of time needed for Gap-Time, it's easy to think you have more time than you actually do. Then you end up like the joke about people who never balance their checkbooks. "I can't be overdrawn—I still have some checks left!" Scheduling Gap-Time is a way of balancing your calendar/time checkbook.

It's easy to see how time-related chaos can, in turn, cause project-related chaos: A lack of Gap-Time can lead to overscheduling and overbooking, often resulting in blown deadlines and derailed projects.

The Right Way to Be Late

For some people, however, the habit of running late may be too hard to break. If this sounds like you or someone you work with, pay attention.

Believe it or not, it's possible to run late considerately. This can be achieved by letting people know up-front about your punctuality problem. Warn them ahead of time by explaining, "I have an unfortunate tendency to run (X) minutes late—please don't take it personally." That way, people will know what to expect, and can choose to do other things with their time than wait, worry, and/or dream up ways to vent their frustration on you when you finally show up. It's also considerate to call ahead when you're running late to let people know when to expect you.

If, however, you're the victim of the "late-ing and waiting game," you need to let Chaos Creators know that the rules have changed—you're in charge now. Tell them that from now on, there's a time limit on how long you will wait (say, 15 minutes), and if they don't show up within that frame of time, you're outta there. Also, be clear about what time your meeting or appointment with them must end—and stick with it.

And if you know you're probably going to be kept waiting by someone, at least be prepared: bring reading materials, paperwork, a snack—anything to help you fill that Gap-Time productively and/or pleasantly.

Timer Therapy

Closely related to insufficient or nonexistent Gap-Time management is Sidetracking. Time-challenged Chaos Creators tend to get sidetracked and wind up in a sort of dreamy, timeless limbo-land. Whether it's talking too long on the phone, schmoozing in the hallway, or stopping to read the articles they're supposed to be filing, the problem is the same: they think time stops for them.

To help stay on track while performing either project or maintenance tasks, a ticking timer (like the one you may have in your kitchen at home) can be a remarkably effective—and even fun—tool. (Inexpensive, too.) Its chief function is to force Chaos Creators to realize that time is ticking by, second by second, instead of stopping for them while they browse, putter, and dither. By setting the timer for short increments (5 to 15 minutes) for the duration of any potentially dawdlesome task—phone calls, filing, sorting through piles of paper—Chaos Creators can gain a more realistic sense of the limits of their time (and perhaps other people's, too).

Of course, it's possible the loud ticking and buzzing noises produced by kitchen-style timers may not be welcomed by others in your workplace, in which case an electronic or digital alarm might be more appropriate. The range of options includes wristwatch alarms, magnetic alarms, and desktop alarms. Many electronic organizers include alarms as well.

Timers are also useful for reminding people when to stop working on a project so they can be on time for an upcoming appointment. There's no mistaking that "Time's up!" sound that only a timer's buzzer can produce. It even provides an element of fun by creating a competitive beat-the-clock sensation. If the Chaos Creators in question are adrenaline addicts who seem to thrive on stress-induced excitement, all the better: The timer may be just the toy they need to make them feel like TV game show contestants.

Chaos Creators afflicted with Treasure Hunt Syndrome are particularly good candidates for such timer therapy. If order is imposed on their chaotic workspace, they may miss the excitement engendered by the thrill of the hunt. But a ticking timer can be used to create an artificial sense of the urgency that they crave.

Setting a short-term goal along with a timer (for example, 30 minutes to complete a clearly defined task) builds pressure, which is released when the timer buzzes. This can induce a special sense of euphoria experienced when a desired result is achieved by organized means. So instead of participating in a crazed (and crazy-making) hurry-flurry-scurry process, Chaos Creators can be more productive without sacrificing too much of the thrilling treasure hunt tension.

Note: If the timer goes off before the goal is achieved, make an educated guess as to the amount of additional time needed to complete the work. Depending on whether your estimate calls for just a few more minutes or more than an hour, you could reset the timer or schedule another block of time for finishing up.

White Space

Another way to deal effectively with Sidetracking is to plan for distractions. The trick is to plan for them without blowing your whole schedule. It's not as tough as it sounds. All you need is a little *white space*.

People who design effective print media ads and Web sites know the value of white space. An effective ad, for example, generally has a good balance of white space (unfilled area), ad copy, and graphics. If an advertisement is cluttered with too many words or images, readers are likely to skip right over it.

Take a look at your time management system or calendar. Does it look like a poorly designed ad, with too many words (commitments) and not enough white space? Although it may seem more efficient to pack your days with side-by-side appointments (and Gap-Time), ultimately it's not as effective as leaving some unfilled time (white space) in your schedule. So make sure to consistently leave white space in your calendar as a buffer between appointments, meetings, deadlines, and so forth.

◆◆◆

> Blocking out white space is the time management equivalent of having overdraft protection on your checking account.

◆◆◆

The difference between Gap-Time and white space is that while Gap-Time helps you be on time for scheduled appointments and meetings, white space helps you stay on track with projects and maintenance work. White space functions as a sort of shock absorber for scheduling bumps caused by distractions, interruptions, emergencies, and delays. It helps you defuse potential schedule bombs, such as when someone dumps a "due yesterday" project on your desk with no warning. White space pumps flexibility into your schedule, and flexibility is one of the keys to effective time management.

Oh, and with that in mind . . . if you're using a paper-based time management system, be sure to write everything in pencil. And don't be afraid to use the eraser, either.

Don't Overlook the Obvious

Quick—if someone asked you to visualize time, what image would come to mind? For many of us, a clock—the kind with "hands" that point to numbers—symbolizes time. For others, it's a calendar.

Which is why I recommend you have one of each, either on or near your desk, right in your sight line. Clocks and calendars are such obvious tools for counteracting chaos, you may have forgotten to make them part of your workspace.

I've found that a clock with a big face gives most people a better sense of time than the digital kind, although it's actually not a bad idea to have both types in your workspace. A large, well-placed calendar may also function as a constant reminder of time. Being face-to-face with a clock and a calendar reduces the possibility of forgetting about time—your own and others'.

Honesty Saves Time

When you're honest with yourself about your limitations, you can be honest with others about your limits. I've found that being up-front and clear about what will and will not work for your schedule often helps prevent chaos. Overbooking and overcommitting frequently occur when people are afraid to admit that they are already overwhelmed by their existing obligations. It's important to remember that you usually have a choice in how you can respond to a request or an assignment, even if the prevailing workplace attitude is "Say yes or say good-bye." Knowing when to say no can save both your schedule and your sanity.

Double-Booking

Sooner or later, despite all your best efforts, you'll probably experience some time-twisting encounters that won't be solved by the previously described solutions. But that doesn't necessarily mean you should concede defeat. It all depends on how creative—or even crafty—you choose to be.

I once had a client who kept rescheduling appointments, often on short notice. She was a Creative Chaos Creator with a great capacity for causing time-related chaos. But because she was actually a person I enjoyed helping, I didn't want to stop working with her.

Observing a pattern in her rescheduling process, I figured out a way to work with it. Her pattern consisted of rescheduling each new appointment once; that is, once she had rescheduled a session, she didn't re-reschedule it. So I began to plan for this seeming inevitability: whenever she called to book an initial appointment, I'd pencil it into my calendar with a question mark next to it. If another client called to request the same time, no problem—I was happy to "double-book," confident that my Rescheduling Queen would be calling just in time. And she always did.

This tactic is a relatively harmless subterfuge that works to counteract time-related chaos. But it's hardly a unique one: Most hotels, airlines, restaurants, and car rental agencies routinely (and usually successfully) double-book reservations. And you can do it too—with caution. I think this tactic should be used mainly as a last-ditch effort only after you've unsuccessfully tried every other way of coping with terminally unreliable Chaos Creators.

My timer just rang. It's time to move on. Soon this chapter will be merely another memory—unless you've already forgotten everything you read. In which case, you definitely need the next chapter.

4

Managing Memory-
Related Chaos

*It's a poor sort of memory that
only works backwards.*

—LEWIS CARROLL

*T*ake a good, hard look at any recent problems you've caused or experienced because of a memory mishap. (By the way, how did you score in the memory portion of the Chaos Questionnaire—or can you even remember?!) Could your memory use a boost? How about your co-workers'?

I was about to make a point, but I've forgotten what it was.

Oh, wait—it's coming back to me.

It's no secret that for many people nowadays, memory is a thing of the past (so to speak). Our memories are overburdened with too much information, too many choices, and too little time for reflection.

Life has become so hectic and complicated, few of us can rely solely on our minds to remember everything we need or want to recall. Even if we could remember everything, what would be the point of wasting so many brain cells? After all, even Albert Einstein supposedly refused to memorize his own phone number because he said he knew where he could look it up! (Of course, he probably would just ask his wife. But it's still a good story.)

Memories Are Made of This

Numerous memory-aiding tools and techniques abound: to-do lists and not-to-do lists; planners and scanners; Pendaflexes and Rolodexes; electronic organizers and computer programs—you name it. And more systems and strategies are being created all the time, because there's just too much to remember without some type of assistance.

People who like to be organized generally understand and accept this reality. And Chaos Conquerors especially enjoy the process of exploring and experimenting with various products and procedures. I know quite a few of these "organizing junkies" who find it fun to keep up with the latest memory-enhancing organizing solutions. (As one of my clients put it, "From now on I'm going to think of organizing as a hobby!" A pretty effective way to maintain the results, in fact.)

But for Chaos Creators, it's another story. Some even stubbornly cling to the idea that "smart people" (such as themselves, of course) should be able to remember everything, and only memory-deficient dummies need to make notes and use systems.

Keep It Simple—Not Simple-Minded

That reminds me of Rowena, a Chaos Creator real estate agent who openly scoffed at my suggestion that she try using a planner to help her remember appointments and follow-up calls. "I keep it all in here," she said smugly, tapping her head. "It's simpler."

Perhaps "simple-minded" would have been more accurate. I found she frequently mixed up her appointments and forgot to handle important details—not wise when you're in a detail-heavy field like real estate. It took more than one self-sabotaged sale to make her reluctantly admit that perhaps my suggestion might be worth trying.

As I pointed out to Rowena, a good system should remember things for you. It supports your mind—so you don't lose your mind! Speaking of which, I've heard many relatively young people jokingly claim they're "going senile" or getting "early Alzheimer's." These youngsters often have great difficulty accepting that their problem isn't so much a lack of memory as a lack of systems and procedures to support the memory.

Memory-challenged Chaos Creators often depend on others to con-

◈ ◈ ◈ ◈ ◈ *Watch-Out Window* ◈ ◈ ◈ ◈ ◈

Some Chaos Creators are experts at manipulating your emotions. They may express admiration for your marvelous memory and, sighing heavily, lament their own shortcomings.

WATCH OUT! These Chaos Creators can flatter you into thinking you have superior memory skills so they can get you to do their remembering for them. Although you may enjoy feeling "gifted" (as I'm sure you are), don't let yourself get caught in this trap. Unless your job duties specifically call for this type of assistance, or you don't mind the extra work, beware! You may find yourself taking on the burdensome role of a workplace "mother."

tinually remind them about everything, from where they put their keys to when they need to be at the airport. They usually forget to write things down; when they do make notes, they're likely to lose them.

Such was the case with Gerri, the Captain Chaos boss in Chapter 1 who had driven her assistant Bill to the verge of quitting. Most of the chaos Gerri caused was due to her overloaded memory and her initial refusal to admit that she had a problem. But once she realized Bill was prepared to make good on his threat to quit, Gerri finally acknowledged her memory-caused mayhem. She told him she was ready to make some changes if he'd agree to help her. Bill was only too happy to oblige.

Both Chaos Creators like Gerri and Chaos Conquerors like Bill may benefit from the memory management tools and tactics that follow.

Interruption Intervention

Here's a typical scenario: You have something in your hand—keys, a file, stapler, whatever—and the phone rings or someone walks in. Your focus shifts to the interruption and before you know it, what you had in your hand a moment ago has vanished like Houdini. You have absolutely no recollection of where you might have put it. A frantic search ensues: it's a full-blown case of Treasure Hunt Syndrome. The seeds of chaos have once again been sown.

"Interruptions are an enemy of the memory-challenged," observes organizing consultant Donna Cowan of Cowan & Company Professional Organizing in San Diego, California.

One technique she recommends for controlling interruptions that can cause memory-related chaos is what she calls "sequencing." Figure out a sequence to follow. For example, when you have something in your hand and an interruption occurs, your sequence might be: 1) Stop; 2) focus; 3) put object next to door (or some other hard-to-miss spot). Identifying one specific place (or "parking lot," as Cowan calls it) where key items can be put during interruptions will cut down on treasure-hunting expeditions.

"Keep in mind that something is always going to try to wedge its way into the sequencing process," Cowan points out. To deal with this inevitability, she suggests a trick she calls "bookmarking": Use a figurative bookmark—actually visualize it—to mentally hold your place when an interruption occurs.

Cowan also recommends legibly labeling frequently misplaced items with their location information so that anyone will know where the materials belong.

V & V vs. Clutter-Mutter

Another memory-boosting tactic is verbalizing and vocalizing (V & V): repeating (aloud, if possible) whatever it is you're afraid of forgetting. This is actually a focusing exercise—it forces you to pay attention, which is really one of the best ways to help your memory. (As Samuel Johnson observed, "The true art of memory is the art of attention.") For example, instead of absently and automatically setting down the stapler you'll be needing again later, make a point of saying—as you set it down— "Stapler on corner of desk" (or wherever you're putting it). When you use V & V, you are imprinting an action on your memory. Even though this process might sound (and feel) somewhat silly, it really does work. Try it and see for yourself. You have nothing to lose—except, perhaps, all those things you've been losing.

Focusing out loud needn't be embarrassing; you can always whisper, or just pretend you're talking to yourself. Treasure hunters are already primed for this; they're used to muttering fitfully as they scramble around looking for the latest misplaced item. "Where is it? Where is it?

◆◆

Out from Under

So you just can't seem to remember where you put something that was in your hand a moment ago. Worse, you haven't been able to find it during a frenzied yet fruitless treasure hunt. But I'll bet I know where it is: underneath something—a larger object that you absent-mindedly placed on top of the smaller item that now eludes you.

Tip: Never—even for a moment—put a bigger thing, such as a binder or a newspaper, on top of a littler thing, such as a disk or a pocket calendar.

◆◆

I know it's here somewhere!" is a popular mantra. I call this symptom clutter-mutter; it's actually the opposite of V & V: instead of helping you focus, it maintains your level of distracted urgency.

Bookmark Your Files

When people borrow files and then forget to return them, chaos happens sooner or later (depending on how soon someone else needs the missing files). If you want to avoid this type of file frenzy, get some Out-Files—files designated to fill the space of borrowed files while simultaneously documenting who borrowed which file, and when. Out-Files are obtainable from various office suppliers, or you can create your own: simply label a manila or colored file "Out-File" and attach a ruled sheet of paper to it, with columns headed "Date Out," "File Name/Category," "Borrower Name," and "Date Returned." The

◆◆◆◆◆◆◆◆◆◆◆◆◆◆◆◆◆◆◆◆◆◆◆◆◆◆◆◆◆◆◆◆◆◆◆◆◆

Not Lost—Just Loaned

If you often forget to return borrowed items—or if others forget to return things to you—here's a quick tip: Any time anything is borrowed or loaned, put a return date reminder note in your calendar (e.g., for one month later). Be sure to include key points—who borrowed what when.

◆◆◆◆◆◆◆◆◆◆◆◆◆◆◆◆◆◆◆◆◆◆◆◆◆◆◆◆◆◆◆◆◆◆◆◆◆

hardest part, of course, is getting Chaos Creators to use the Out-Files properly and consistently. Establishing and enforcing this rule may take some doing. In the meantime, you might want to keep your file drawers locked up if you have that option.

Memory Management Methods of the Rich and Famous

One of the most effective methods overall for memory management is cheap, convenient, and low-tech—and many rich and highly successful business people absolutely swear by it. It's called "writing it down," and almost anyone can do it.

Billionaire Richard Branson, founder of the Virgin business empire, neither types nor uses a computer. Instead, as he writes in *Losing My Virginity*, ". . . my most essential possession is a standard-sized school notebook . . . I carry this everywhere . . ." Branson uses a notebook (he now has a bookcase full of ones he's filled up) to make notes of everything—reminders, phone conversations, comments made to him in person, to-do lists. This frees his mind for deal-making. Why waste brain cells on mundane memory matters when you can be focusing on making your next billion?

Likewise, Lillian Vernon, founder and CEO of one of the most successful mail order companies, is known for her habit of taking notes. "Once I write something down," she says in *An Eye for Winners*, "I don't have to worry about remembering it. That saves mental energy, and I can concentrate on something else." The "something else" she's able to concentrate on is invariably profitable.

You might want to make a note of that. If you remember just one thing—keep something to write with and a notebook handy—you won't have to remember anything else.

One more low-tech tool: For capturing phone messages and other to-do reminder notes, a carbonless-copy message book can be a sanity-saver. You can tear off the top copy of a note or message, lose it, and still have a permanent record in the spiral-bound book. Thwart more chaos: Use a long string to tie a pen to the spiral, and you'll have one less thing to lose.

To Do or Not to Do

Both note-taking and list-making can be good memory management techniques. Combine them, and you've got the most familiar type of reminder list: the to-do list. But despite its apparent popularity, many people complain that to-do lists are a problem for them. I think I know why. You see, in my line of work, I get to look at a lot of to-do lists—my clients often ask for advice on how to do their to-do's. And I've noticed a common flaw in the way most of these lists are composed.

A typical to-do list tends to include a variety of unrelated reminders; for example:

1. Write thank you.
2. Reorganize filing system.
3. Set up database.

Number 4 might as well be: Become a neurosurgeon.

The only thing these four items have in common is that they're all described in just three words. This conciseness actually serves a useful purpose: it makes it easier to move them from list to list—forever. Which is exactly what happens with major projects (such as items 2 and 3 on the above list) because they rarely get done. And that's the main reason most people complain about their to-do lists.

If you are tired of moving reminders from list to list, here's my advice. First, try categorizing your to-do lists so you don't end up lumping all these unrelated tasks together. You can use the Master List Form which follows, or create your own version if you prefer. The point is to group similar tasks; this will make it easier for you to see which ones are maintenance work and which are projects.

Next, break down projects, such as "Reorganize filing system," into smaller steps. (By the way, if you really do plan to reorganize your filing system, those steps are provided in Chapter 6.) It's like the old riddle. Question: How do you eat an elephant? Answer: One bite at a time. Breaking down your larger to-do's into bite-sized pieces will make almost any project more doable, and just might prevent *you* from breaking down instead.

Finally, pencil in a time estimate next to each task or project step. If you have trouble coming up with time estimates, just put down "2

Master List Form

CALLS

CORRESPONDENCE/TO SEND

PROJECTS/TO DO

ERRANDS/TO RUN

TO ORDER/TO OBTAIN

MISCELLANEOUS

◆◆

Overcoming Overwhelm

The "one bite at a time" method is also effective for overcoming Overwhelm, a nervous condition often brought on by overloaded memory and characterized by paralysis of the decision-making muscles. Basically, Overwhelm occurs when you become paralyzed by possibilities. If you are in the throes of an Overwhelm attack—it can come on quite suddenly—sit down and take a few deep breaths (don't forget to exhale). Then make a step-by-step list of whatever you absolutely must get done within the next hour. (And don't waste time arguing that you don't have the time to do this. If you have time to panic, then you have enough time to make a little list.) *Focus only on your most immediate must-do's.* You'll feel your brain unfreezing as you proceed.

◆◆

hours." At least it's a start; you can always change it later. The main thing is to get yourself in the habit of thinking about how much time you need to schedule in order to get your to-do's done. Doing this will make your to-do lists work more effectively for you. And since these lists help to support your memory, this is advice worth remembering.

Memorable Mini-Marvels

Some people find gadgets more fun to use and harder to lose than paper-based systems. Pocket-size electronic organizers, handheld computers such as the Palm Pilot, and tiny recorders may be options worth exploring for those who just won't write things down, or who lose what they do write. These mini-marvels are constantly being improved and upgraded; therefore, I'll only provide a general overview here of this category of products. For more current information, keep a look out for product reviews on the Web or in magazines.

At the risk of sounding sexist, I've found that men are more likely than women to use electronic gadgets and gizmos. It seems to be one of those "guy things." Be that as it may, almost anyone of either gender may benefit from the pocket- and purse-sized, battery-operated organizer and recorder options that have become increasingly streamlined and affordable.

Handheld computers allow you to "write" or draw directly on the screen with a cordless stylus. They contain many of the same features as electronic organizers, including the ability to interface with computers. This type of product may appeal to people who tend to write things down on little scraps of paper and then lose them.

Electronic organizers—also called "personal productivity tools"— have been described as a cross between a pocket calculator and a laptop computer. They range from tiny baubles the size of a business card to chunky checkbook-size devices. If you're a gadget person, such products may be worth a try, especially since most of them have money-back guarantees.

Perhaps the best-known electronic organizer is the Sharp Wizard, rated tops by *Consumer Reports*. Similar products include Casio Executive B.O.S.S. and Rolodex Pocket Electrodex. Most provide at least 10 features, namely:

1. Alarm (linked to an appointment scheduler)
2. Business card file
3. Calculator
4. Calendar
5. Clock
6. Computer link
7. Memo pad
8. Memory cards
9. Password protection
10. Phone book

Like any multi-featured electronic gadget, organizers take time and effort to master. It's always easier to buy one than to take the time to learn how to use it. Many a Wizard has languished in K-Oz (pardon the pun), relegated to a drawer cluttered with defunct devices and dashed dreams.

So how do you make sure this doesn't happen? Try this: If the idea of using an electronic organizer seems appealing but you're concerned about whether you or your Chaos Creators will ever actually figure out how to use it, do some homework. Read the instructions (at least for the basic functions) and then offer to show your colleagues how it works.

Teaching others is sometimes the best way to learn a new skill yourself. Be enthusiastic without being overpowering, and don't forget to emphasize both the benefits and the fun of using it.

By the way, the above tactic worked well for Bill. He showed Gerri how to use a Sharp Wizard, and eventually it helped whittle down her chaos-causing ways.

Another tactic: If your Chaos Creators are know-it-alls, ask them to show you how it works; then they'll be forced to learn it themselves.

Your Voice Brings Back Memories . . .

Less complicated than electronic organizers but equally handy, digital voice recorders are an ideal solution for those who find it too much trouble to jot down a reminder to themselves. As of this writing, several brands are available. Here are a few examples:

♦ The Olympus V-90 records for 90 minutes, fits in the palm of your hand, and runs on one AAA battery.

♦ The Executive Voice Organizer has more features, including a 512K memory and an LCD screen for displaying phone numbers (it can hold up to 400) or other information you can access simply by speaking into it. It also has a reminder function for appointments.

♦ The FlashBack Digital Recorder comes with a removable, reusable 30-minute SoundClip. When the 30 minutes of recording time are used up, the previous messages can either be recorded over or removed (via the SoundClip) and stored indefinitely, since the SoundClip is replaceable. Because this device has only two buttons, ergonomically designed, it can be operated with just one hand, even while driving or in the dark.

By the time you read this, I'll bet there will be voice memo devices small enough to be worn as nose-rings and powerful enough to hold a year's worth of messages. But even if the current gizmos are as good as they're gonna get, they still can be pretty useful for helping reduce memory-related chaos.

Don't Turn the Page . . . Yet

Another option worth exploring is a paging system. Instead of the basic numeric pagers that only allow callers to key in a phone number which then appears on the pager display, consider using alphanumeric pagers. They have the capacity to display not just the phone number but an entire message on the pager screen. So whether it's you or someone else who needs to be reminded regularly, pagers can come in handy. (If the Chaos Creators in question are particularly absentminded, I'd recommend having the pager surgically attached.)

Okay, now you can turn the page. Especially if you're ready to find out how to control communication-related chaos.

5

Controlling Communication- Related Chaos

Excuse me for not answering your letter sooner, but I've been so busy not answering letters that I couldn't get around to not answering yours in time.

—GROUCHO MARX

*N*owadays, "you've got mail" can mean you've got anything from good old-fashioned "snail mail" to e-mail to voice mail, not to mention faxes and overnight postal services. "Phone" may refer to the one on your desk, the one in your pocket, the one in your car, or the one wrapped around your head. Then there's pagers and teleconferencing and . . . and . . . Hello? Hello? Are you there? I hope we didn't get cut off—I had a point to make!

You'd think our access to all these different communication tools would have caused miscommunication to become extinct (or at least land it on the endangered list). Instead, the plethora of options has helped miscommunication multiply and mutate. Every wonderful new communication tool doubles

From Confusion to Chaos

According to a study by Accountemps, a personnel agency, the average company employee spends the equivalent of two months out of every year dealing with problems caused by his or her own or others' distorted communication patterns.

as a miscommunication tool, providing Chaos Creators with fresh opportunities to cause chaos.

One of the best ways to counteract this type of chaos is by *consistently making a conscious effort to communicate effectively*. Effective communication occurs when at least two people are involved in an exchange of messages and each participant ends up with a fairly good understanding of what the other has communicated. This should be your goal every time you communicate, whether you are

- ♦ Sending an e-mail

- ♦ Leaving a voice mail message

- ♦ Faxing a note

- ♦ Composing a letter, memo, report, article, etc.

- ♦ Having a discussion with someone on the phone or in person

- ♦ Speaking to an audience

- ♦ Training or teaching

- ♦ Conducting or participating in a meeting

Babble and Grunt

The problem is, communicating effectively doesn't come naturally—which may be why it is such a rare occurrence. It's so much easier to either babble away thoughtlessly or issue only occasional grunts, depending on your preferred style. By contrast, effective communication takes effort; it's actually another organizing process. Not as easy as babbling or grunting, perhaps, but ultimately far more beneficial to all concerned.

The hallmarks of effective communication are what I call the Five C's—clarity, conciseness, comprehension, completeness, and consideration. These are the qualities that help prevent and counteract misassumptions, misunderstandings, mistakes, confusion, contradictions, disputes . . . all kinds of communication-related chaos. The Five C's apply to every form of communication—and when any one of them is lacking, an opportunity for chaos can arise.

Here are four steps to help you achieve the Five C's.

FOUR STEPS TO EFFECTIVE COMMUNICATION

1. Ask people which method of communication they prefer—and use it consistently when contacting them, unless it proves ineffective. Be sure to let others know the best ways to reach you, too.

Most of us have two types of communication methods—preferred and deferred. For example, I prefer voice mail or fax, and defer e-mail. I always let people know that I tend to respond within 24 hours to both voice mail and fax communications, but more slowly to e-mail. (I use e-mail mostly for communicating with people who prefer it to other forms of contact.) What dictates whose preferred method takes precedence? That depends on the situation. In general, however, the person who has initiated the exchange of messages or who is depending on a response should use the other person's preferred method.

If you've been having trouble getting various people to respond to your communication efforts, perhaps the problem is that you're not using their preferred method(s). Worse, you may actually be attempting to contact them in ways they find inappropriate—or even annoying. For example, some people hate to receive a fax unless it is, in their opinion, urgent. Repeatedly faxing non-urgent material to such a person practically guarantees a cold shoulder instead of a warm response.

On the other hand, communicating effectively with certain people may entail *not* using their favorite method. For example, people who love to talk can end up keeping you on the phone too long if you let them. (Later in this chapter I'll offer tips for dealing with these "Phone-o-holics.")

Because people may not be consciously aware of their communication preferences and dislikes, you might need to experiment with different "contactics" for different situations: If e-mailing someone has proved futile, try calling instead; if leaving voice mail messages hasn't been effective, see whether faxing works better, and so forth. Be resourceful.

2. Prepare an agenda or a prioritized checklist that includes each point you need to cover in your communication.

The most highly accomplished and famously effective communicators routinely do this, so why shouldn't you? Don't delude yourself into thinking you can wing it; such hubris often sows the seeds of chaos.

Creating and following an agenda—an outline for an organized sequence of topics—can help you communicate more clearly, concisely, and completely by:

♦ Ensuring you won't forget key points and crucial details.
♦ Giving you a plan to follow so your communication process can proceed in an effective order. Since communication is at least a two-way process, an agenda should be flexible enough to accommodate more than just your own interests and concerns. (Otherwise "having your own agenda" can take on a darker meaning.)
♦ Letting you be both focused and relaxed during the communication process. (You can pay more attention to what others are saying if your brain's not buzzing away trying to remember what you're supposed to cover.)

The sequenced structure provided by an agenda differentiates it from a prioritized checklist. Agenda sequencing—like the sequencing technique described in Chapter 4—involves finding a way to connect topics so that they flow together sequentially (e.g., beginning-middle-end); prioritizing means listing things in order of importance (e.g., first, second, third). You need to use your judgment about which format you want to use for any given communication. It depends on the circumstances. A prioritized checklist—or even just an itemized one—is often sufficient for quickie communications such as voice mail messages; an agenda format may work better for detail-heavy situations such as committee meetings and project outlines.

Another difference between agendas and prioritized checklists is the amount of time it takes to prepare them. List making requires less planning and therefore takes less time than sequencing. Composing an agenda is a three-step process. Depending on the number of things you want to cover, this might take anywhere from under five minutes to over an hour. If this seems like too much time, remember that an effective agenda will, in the long run, save you a lot more time by helping to prevent chaos. (*Note:* If you just don't have enough time left to create an agenda before an important communication deadline, at least make a list.)

To compose effective agendas, follow these sequencing steps:

♦ Do a "brain dump," jotting down (or recording, or keying in) anything you can think of that you might want to cover in your communication.

♦ Go back over your notes and group similar topics or points together. Delete any redundant or unnecessary material.

♦ Organize your topics or points into a logical sequence (beginning-middle-end). Be sure to include some white space for any points that the other participants may wish to discuss.

♦ If appropriate, include a time estimate for each agenda topic.

3. **During any simultaneously interactive communication process (e.g., conversation, meeting, training session), make a point of periodically monitoring comprehension levels.**

Try not to assume either that you are being understood or that you are understanding others. I recommend three techniques that help aid and monitor comprehension:

Clarifying: Do not hesitate to question unclear or incomplete instructions, suggestions, requests, or directives. For example, someone states that he needs to have some materials from you in "two weeks." But two weeks means different things to different people. Is it two weeks from today? Or does he mean the Friday of next week? Or perhaps the Monday of the following week? Does he need it by a certain time of day, say, 9 A.M.? noon? midnight? Unless you eliminate the guesswork and push for clarity on points like this, chaos is sure to follow.

Mirroring: Repeat back instructions, etc., issued by the other person; any gaps or misunderstandings surface immediately and can then be corrected. Always offer to do this first, both to demonstrate the mirroring technique and to ensure that you are accurately hearing others. Say something like: "I'm going to repeat back to you what I thought I heard you say just to make sure I got it right." Afterwards, when applicable, encourage others to mirror anything you've said that you think they may have misunderstood.

Recapping: Periodically sum up the main points of the communication as it progresses, both as speaker and as listener. Be alert for appropriate times to do this—when wrapping up a topic segment, for example.

4. **Practice being an effective receiver of communications (that is, being a good listener and reader).**

There's no substitute for paying attention. This means focusing on what a person is communicating, instead of letting your mind drift or race ahead. (*Note:* This applies to written as well as spoken communication.) With regard to spoken communication, remember that listening involves more than just waiting until it's your turn to speak, and far more than merely adopting the pose of a good listener (e.g., direct eye contact, leaning forward, making encouraging "mm-hmm" sounds).

Being a good listener involves being both receptive and interactive. This means politely interrupting a long-winded speaker so you can ask questions (e.g., when someone is giving incomplete information or instructions) or refocusing a discussion that has drifted off course. Likewise, when people talk too fast for you to follow them, it's your responsibility to speak up; tactfully interrupt to let them know that you're trying to listen carefully and you need their cooperation. Ultimately, interactive listening helps you make sure that communication gaps get filled. (*Note:* You need to be an interactive listener to utilize the techniques mentioned in Step 3.)

Four Ways to Miscommunicate

Now that we've covered effective communication techniques, let's look at what happens when people *don't* use them. Here are the most common ways in which Chaos Creators miscommunicate.

♦ *Keeping quiet.* Getting some of them to communicate is like pulling teeth. They rarely return phone calls, avoid answering correspondence, and/or may barely speak in person. But is it *their* fault you're not a mind reader? Of course not.

♦ *Being long-winded.* Others talk too much, especially on the phone or in meetings; on paper or e-mail, they'll go on and on. Either way, they take ages to get to the point. Then they blame you for not being able to follow their ramblings.

♦ *Double-talking.* They're consistently unclear, yet somehow manage to blame you for "misunderstanding" them. Whether in meet-

◆◆

What Was That You Just Said?

Don't rule out the possibility that some communication-related chaos might have a physical basis. For example, hearing impairment could be at the root of ongoing misunderstandings and miscommunication.

If you think hearing impairment is a possible problem for you or someone else, help is just a phone call away. Call 800-222-3277 for an FDA-approved Dial-a-Hearing Screening Test, or contact a hearing center in your area.

◆◆

ings or one-on-one, whether purposely or otherwise, they manage to keep others continually confused.

◆ *Not listening.* They invariably misunderstand what you say, no matter how clear you try to be. But of course, the problem is all your fault—at least as far as they're concerned.

Phone-o-phobes

Faxes, e-mail, and "snail mail" have their uses, but inevitably there comes a time when you've got to actually "reach out and touch someone," as those old telephone commercials used to warble. And if that someone is a Phone-o-phobe, good luck.

Phone-o-phobes are people who consistently fail to return phone calls. The Phone-o-phobe population appears to be increasing faster than the federal deficit. In fact, it's become so rare to have your call returned promptly—if at all—that when it happens you may go into shock and forget why you left a message in the first place.

No one likes to have their calls ignored. Many people even perceive it (consciously or subconsciously) as a sign of disrespect. But I believe that in most cases, the only "dissing" involved is disorganization.

If you're a Phone-o-phobe, think about the lack of consideration others perceive when you fail to return phone calls. Is that the way you want to be viewed? Is this an effective business technique? Probably not. (Unless, of course, you work in Hollywood.)

◆◆

If there is an afterlife,
I guess I'd use it to return phone calls.

—FRAN LEBOWITZ

◆◆

Certainly, there are times—and valid reasons—to not return various calls. Messages from people trying to sell you something you don't want, or from someone who is harassing you in some way, often do not warrant a response. Then there are those callers who you know from experience are extremely inconsiderate of your time, or who always seem to want something from you yet never reciprocate. (Avoiding *them* is actually a survival technique.) And sometimes you're just not able to respond due to circumstances beyond your control. But there's a big difference between occasionally choosing not to return specific calls and consistently neglecting to do so.

Some Phone-o-phobes don't take or return calls simply because the phone is not their preferred method of communication, as discussed earlier. They may prefer e-mail or find it easier to jot a note and fax it; they just don't "do phone." If this sounds like you, then it's your professional duty to let people know how you prefer to be contacted so they're not wasting time trying to reach you by phone.

Perhaps you shy away from identifying yourself as a Phone-o-phobe. That's normal. As with other chaos-causing behaviors, it's much easier to spot other people's phone-o-phobic tendencies than it is to notice your own. But if you completed Part I of the Chaos Questionnaire and checked the "Frequently" box for questions 11 and 12, you can call yourself a Phone-o-phobe. (Just don't be surprised if you don't get around to calling yourself back.)

If you think your habit of being perpetually unavailable to callers implies that you are some type of VIP—you're right! VIP = Very Inconsiderate Phone-o-phobe. Stop deluding yourself. The fact is, the most successful people are often sticklers for answering their own phones and returning calls promptly.

Example: A 1999 *New Yorker* profile of legendary Wall Street figure Alan "Ace" Greenberg, the billionaire chairman of the investment firm Bear Stearns, described his "fanaticism about being accessible and promptly responsive to callers." According to the article, Greenberg often answers his own phone despite having two assistants. The length of an average conversation? "About ten seconds."

To overcome your phone-o-phobic tendencies, try:

♦ Thinking of your phone as a tool—like your pen or your Post-Its—that you employ for specific purposes. You don't need to have it stuck to your ear all day. You just need to use it enough to get your job done and not alienate others.

♦ Utilizing a system that reminds you to return calls. You can use something simple such as a telephone message book with carbonless copies or a more high-tech option like an electronic organizer. (Both of these are described in more detail in Chapter 4).

♦ Setting aside time each day for returning calls. (Remember your Maintenance Time Worksheet?) You could make it your first task of the day, or your last—or maybe somewhere in the middle, depending on what works best for you. Whichever you choose, pencil that time into your schedule as a maintenance activity.

Phone-o-phobe—or Not?

In some instances, a person who refuses to return your calls may not be a Phone-o-phobe; he or she is simply avoiding *you* (not everyone) for whatever reason. Stop a moment and consider whether there is even the tiniest possibility that you may be contributing to the problem in some way.

♦ Do you express yourself clearly, or mumble unintelligibly?

♦ Are your messages concise, or do you tend to be long-winded?

♦ Are your messages well-organized, or do you ramble?

♦ Do you sound upbeat, or have you acquired the dreaded "drone tone"?

♦ Do you always include the best times and ways to reach you, or just expect others to track you down?

Then again, it may not be your fault after all. It's common for people to avoid returning calls when they don't want to relate unexpected or unpleasant news, or if they don't have something ready for you (promised information or answers).

Whether or not these possibilities contain any glimmer of truth, if you follow the Five P's, below, you'll be able to increase communication while reducing your frustration level.

The Five P's for Dealing Effectively with Phone-o-phobes (and Everyone Else Too)

1. ***Be prepared.*** Before you pick up the phone to make an important call, take a moment to prepare a checklist (described earlier) of what it is you need to convey and/or what information you need to get. It's always wise to clarify your objective and do some planning prior to taking any action, and phone calls are no exception. This way you'll be ready to either speak directly and effectively with your contact or leave a "C-worthy" message.

2. ***Be precise.*** When leaving a message, be sure it includes three specific points, expressed clearly and concisely: *purpose*—why you are calling; *deadline*—by when you need to hear back; and *availability*—the best times and methods for reaching you (including whether it's okay for them to respond via voice mail, e-mail, or fax). It's also a good idea to clearly state your name and contact number both at the beginning and end of your message.

3. ***Be provocative.*** Although it's important to be specific about certain aspects of your message, it can also be effective to be a little mysterious about other points. This is especially true if you'd prefer to speak directly with someone instead of just getting a message back. By implying that you have news of import to impart, a compliment to pass along, a useful bit of information, or juicy gossip to share, you may be able to entice an otherwise reluctant Phone-o-phobe into calling you back. (This trick has worked for multilevel marketers for years.) Be sure to have something you can use to back up your tease, or this tactic could backfire.

4. ***Be pleasant.*** It's easy to get angry when you've left messages repeatedly that languish unreturned in an overstuffed voice mailbox or on an overflowing desk. But do your best to control both your

tone of voice and your choice of words when you call yet again. A pleasant-sounding voice conveying a message that displays a rueful sense of humor generally will get better results than if you leave an angry, accusatory dispatch.

5. *Be persistent.* One of my first jobs out of college was as a bill collector. I learned that to get results in most cases, all I had to do was keep following up. (I rarely had to break anyone's legs.) This skill has stood me in good stead, especially when dealing with Phone-o-phobes. But persistence is most effective when you follow a pattern: Whenever I leave messages, I always mention that if I don't hear back by a certain date or time, I'll call again. Then I mark the "calls" section of my daily planner to remind me to follow up if necessary—and I always call again if I haven't heard back by that time or date. Sooner or later Phone-o-phobes discover that there's no escape from me; either I reach them or they give up and call me back. This strategy takes effort and organization, but it gets results. (For peak persistence performance, techie types might want to try a contact management software program such as ACT! by Symantec. Contact managers, as they are called, remind you with alarms when to make follow-up calls and also include a variety of related useful features.)

Telephone Tag, Anyone?

Some of my best phone conversations have been with people I've never talked to. I maintain several effective and mutually beneficial business relationships primarily through exchanges of voice mail messages. This saves us all time because leaving messages tends to be quicker than actually talking directly to each other.

You could say I'm the captain of a telephone tag team.

That's why I don't understand when others say they "hate playing telephone tag." (Then again, they're referring to the only sport at which I truly excel.) What I think these people really mean is that they hate ineffective message exchanges.

To make yours more effective, I recommend establishing your purpose before making a call to someone's message system. Is your goal to . . .

- ◆ Actually speak to a live human being?

- ◆ Get points for attempting to return a call?

- ◆ Get a call back with specific information?

- ◆ Just be a pest?

The last item listed is the goal easiest to inadvertently achieve. If you'd prefer to eliminate this possibility, reread item 2 of the Five P's. Follow those instructions and you'll win at phone tag every time.

Voice Mail Tips

- ◆ When talking to voice mail, don't be afraid to use any available options for listening to your message; then you can delete and re-record until you're satisfied with it. I often do this because I've noticed I leave a clearer, more streamlined message on my second or third try. It's worth the extra time because it can save more time later by eliminating potential communication-related chaos.

- ◆ If you want to encourage others to leave effective messages on your voice mail, include clear instructions on your outgoing message. The "Be Precise" suggestions (#2 of the Five P's) can be used for this purpose. Try to keep offered options (such as delete and re-record) as simple as possible.

Phone-o-holics

At the opposite end of the spectrum from Phone-o-phobes are Phone-o-holics—people who love to talk on the phone. This topic always reminds me of Margie, a disorganized administrative assistant at a literary agency. Her outgoing manner and quick laugh charmed everyone she spoke with on the phone. Little did they know that while she was cheerily chatting away with them, she was also attempting—often unsuccessfully—to handle several other tasks. Filing, mail processing, answering correspondence, sending faxes— Margie tried to juggle it all while yakking away.

But successful multitasking takes strong focusing and organizational skills, which Margie lacked. So inevitably, her phone-o-holic tendency began to take its toll on the office's operations. She kept falling behind in her work and often made chaos-causing mistakes, such as the time she sent a fax with confidential information to the wrong person. This incident almost cost the company two clients, and Chaos Cadet Margie nearly lost her job.

If you suspect you have phone-o-holic tendencies, you may want to:

◆◆◆◆◆◆◆◆◆◆◆◆◆◆◆◆◆◆◆◆◆◆◆◆◆◆◆◆◆◆◆◆◆◆◆

Phoning + Filing = Chaos

Even Chaos Conquerors can get distracted and make chaos-causing errors if they attempt certain tasks while talking on the phone. It's easy to misfile a document or mis-address an envelope when you're engaged in conversation. I learned this lesson myself one day after I almost went crazy looking for a particular document that I thought needed to be filed. After several frantic minutes of searching (during which I experienced a surge of empathy for my clients), I had a memory flash: I'd already filed the paper earlier that day . . . while talking on the phone. When I checked the file, sure enough, there it was, right where it belonged. Which just goes to show— sometimes being efficient ain't all it's cracked up to be.

◆◆◆◆◆◆◆◆◆◆◆◆◆◆◆◆◆◆◆◆◆◆◆◆◆◆◆◆◆◆◆◆◆◆◆

- ◆ Set a timer as a reminder to limit the length of your calls.

- ◆ On outgoing communication, use fax or e-mail to cut down on excess dialogue.

- ◆ Make a list of key points to cover in important calls, and stick with it. This is easier to do when leaving a voice mail message, but it can also work during live interactions.

- ◆ Discipline yourself to concentrate on one task at a time. For example, if you've got another important task to do, have an assistant or voice mail handle incoming calls for you until you're free.

❖ ❖ ❖ ❖ ❖   *Watch-Out Window*   ❖ ❖ ❖ ❖ ❖

Perhaps you're thinking, don't all these phone call rules just serve to make conversation stilted and awkward? What's wrong with a little spontaneity? Why should talking on the phone need to be strategized?

WATCH OUT! You're missing the point. Spontaneity is great (as long as it's planned out well in advance) if you don't have a track record of creating the types of communication-related chaos we've been discussing. But if you have demonstrated any Phone-o-holic tendencies, it's time to start listening more and talking less. Do whatever you can do to stay focused. Remember, focus is the enemy of chaos—and vice versa.

If on the other hand, you're dealing with a colleague who is a Phone-o-holic, you probably have fewer options. These may include:

♦ If you're in a position to affect policy, you could establish a rule to limit phone time on a per-call basis; and/or establish a rule that certain tasks (e.g., filing, faxing, mail sorting) cannot be performed simultaneously with phone calls. In the case of someone like Margie, this might be your best bet.

♦ For other situations, obtaining hands-free phone equipment such as the HelloSet Pro headset (see Appendix A) may enable your Phone-o-holic to function somewhat more effectively.

The Write Stuff

I once received an eye-catching, expensive-looking announcement about an upcoming seminar on "how to market your business." At least I assumed it was upcoming. I couldn't really tell because, while this sales piece detailed everything from the speaker's impressive credentials to the four different payment options, one small but crucial bit of information was missing: the date.

What would you call a mistake like this: careless? stupid? sloppy? How about—none of the above? In seeking the root of this chaos-causing error, I observed that the brochure was carefully (not carelessly) thought out; cleverly (not stupidly) illustrated; and elegantly (not sloppily) composed. What's more, the writing was clear and concise, and the attached registration form was considerately designed: easy to use, with fill-in blanks spacious enough to accommodate a real person's writing. (I hate poorly designed forms with tiny little slots.) Overall, it was a well-done piece. Too bad it lacked one of the crucial Five C's—completeness.

Have you noticed how common this type of error has become? I certainly have. I keep getting things like meeting notices that lack starting times, event invitations with no phone number (but with pleas for RSVPs!), fundraising requests without return addresses, and press releases devoid of contact information. And I've heard of many other examples.

When you leave out something important, you leave room for chaos. How can you avoid making this kind of miscommunication mistake? It's actually quite simple, once you know which rules to follow.

Rules for Chaos-Free Written Communication

1. **The Journalists' Rule.** Make sure your communication covers the basics—what journalists call the Five W's: Who, what, when, where, and why. Whenever possible, include these key points in the first paragraph. In many cases, anything more is superfluous, while anything less has great potential for causing chaos. Ensure completeness by always double-checking written communications against the Five W's.

   Tip: You might want to post a Five W's reminder note in your sight line. (Too bad that marketing expert with the fancy brochure didn't think of this.)

2. **The Department of Redundancy Department's Rule.** Don't make the mistake of confusing redundancy with completeness. And be sure to avoid the error of confusing completeness with redundancy—and vice versa. (See what I mean?)

   Tip: After making sure you've covered your Five W's (also known as "covering your *a*'s"), check for redundancy by scanning (or computer-checking) your written communication carefully to spot overuse of key words or their variations.

Example: For example, avoid repeatedly repetitive repetition, such as this example. (See what I mean—again?)

3. The Anti-anti-completeness (aka Unnecessary Complexity) Rule. Don't confuse complicated with complete, either. It's common to pile on so many details that you lose sight of a document's purpose or priorities.

Example: If your intention is to obfuscate an issue, distract others from something, show off all the multisyllabic words in your vocabulary, or just demonstrate a talent for creating unnecessarily long or complex sentences—sort of like this one—then go right ahead. Or, just be verbose.

Tip: Try to stay as close to the Five W's as possible. Break down complex concepts into smaller segments (like the "one bite at a time" technique described in Chapter 4); wherever appropriate, use a bulleted-list format to delineate key points.

The Check's in the Mail (Yeah, sure)

Let's say your written communications are consistently clear, concise, comprehensible, and complete. Four out of the Five C's—pretty impressive, right? Yes. But sufficient to ensure effective communication? That depends on whether you ever actually send anything out to anyone.

The fifth C, consideration, can really mean the difference between communication and chaos. So far, we've covered a variety of techniques reflecting considerate behavior, including asking others for their preferred methods of communication; curbing both phone-o-phobic and phone-o-holic tendencies; and being an interactive listener. But there's one more area in which consideration is especially important: answering mail and sending promised or expected materials.

One of the best ways to demonstrate consideration is to follow through on what you've promised to do—and when you can't, to let everyone involved know in enough time so they can make adjustments in their plans if necessary. It's simply inconsiderate to leave people waiting and wondering what happened to the purchase order or the estimate you claimed you were sending two weeks ago; or whether you ever received their request for materials last month.

If you completed Part I of the Chaos Questionnaire and checked "Frequently" for questions 13 and 14, then you already know you're guilty of this chaos-causing behavior. The single most important thing you can do to counteract it is this: use your Maintenance Time Worksheet from Chapter 3 to help you plan daily or weekly maintenance time for correspondence and related tasks; block out time in your calendar for this purpose.

Depending on the line of work you're in and your position, you might also want to:

♦ Use a date-stamper to mark incoming items so you'll know when you received them; also note the date a response is sent, if applicable.

♦ Keep your "correspondence to be answered" together by setting up a holding place or paper-flow system (described in Chapter 6), and group any necessary supplies nearby.

♦ Set up a correspondence log to document outgoing and/or incoming correspondence.

♦ Follow up to make sure correspondence and other materials you send have been received and/or are being handled.

Minimizing Meeting Mayhem

As some wit once said, "Meetings are where you keep minutes and lose hours." If you perceive yourself as the Chaos Creator whose meetings take forever and go nowhere, I suggest that you:

♦ Decide on a meeting goal: you need to know exactly what you hope to accomplish.

♦ Create an agenda (see Step 2 from "Four Steps to Effective Communication"); be sure to put time estimates next to each agenda topic.

♦ Give yourself and the attendees the goal as well as a projected time by which you expect the meeting to be over; invite the others to remind you if the discussion digresses unproductively.

♦ Afterward, ask a trusted colleague who was present at the meeting to give you feedback on how well you did in sticking to the subject, meeting your deadline, and achieving the stated goal.

If you're the victim instead of the creator of the chaos, your options may be more limited depending on the workplace roles occupied by you and the meeting meister. But you can, at the very least:

♦ Ask that the purpose of the meeting be clarified at the outset of each meeting.

♦ Set ground rules to maintain focus and order—and speak up whenever anyone starts circumnavigating.

If a weekly or monthly meeting always drags on too long, speak to the person who either sets up or directs the meeting. Volunteer to be a timekeeper or to take the minutes. Then you'll have license to interrupt digressors and request clarification from the communication bunglers.

Bruce Breier, president of BHB Consulting Services in La Jolla, California, has facilitated hundreds of meetings during his 23-year career as an organizational consultant. "I have three non-negotiable protocol points for group meetings," he says. "One, agenda's mandatory—no agenda, no meeting. Two, start on time. And three, end on time." Breier also emphasizes the importance of beginning the wrap-up process 5 to 10 minutes before the stated ending time.

"Remember the five-minute warning bell in school?" says Breier. "You need to have that equivalent for meetings, so people can make the transition to their next commitment without stress." And, he adds, the time *not* to start a new topic is a few minutes before a meeting is supposed to end. "That's not only inefficient," Breier observes, "but also discourteous and insensitive."

A Word About E-mail

Breier also has some cogent comments about controlling e-mail chaos. "Most companies lack effective guidelines for employees to utilize e-mail," he says. "They need to know that it's not supposed to be like a chat room." He also recommends:

♦ Using office e-mail primarily for non-urgent requests that don't require same-day responses. For questions that need quicker answers, leave a voice mail message specifying that you'd like a response that same day.

♦ Dealing with e-mail daily. "It's becoming more and more critical to allocate time for e-mail maintenance," Breier points out. Reply, save, and delete (preferably more of the latter).

E-mail may be an efficient way to exchange information, but that also makes it an efficient way to miscommunicate. Its speed of usage fosters sloppy, unclear writing; many people don't bother reading over a message they've just keyed in, preferring to hit "Send" and move on. And the sheer volume of e-mail causes many recipients to skim messages so quickly that they miss important details.

That's why clarity and conciseness are especially crucial for effective e-mail communication. To achieve those two C's, limit e-mails to one topic, and make sure all key points are covered in the first paragraph. Many busy people don't read past those first few sentences. So whatever you do, keep it brief. The whole point of e-mail is that it's a quick way to communicate. Don't bog down your message with excess detail. (*Note:* For details on deleting details, see "Rules for Chaos-Free Written Communication.")

Between the Five C's, the Five P's, and the Five W's, your communication-related chaos episodes should be history. At the very least, you'll have some of your consonants in order.

By now I hope you've started to see how the different types of chaos cures are actually interconnected. Some communication tools, such as e-mail, can double as timesavers; others, such as telephone message books, are memory-helpers. Likewise, memory-bolstering lists help you manage your time, while time management systems can support your memory.

In the next chapter, you'll discover how information-related chaos is linked to the previously described chaos categories and cures, and vice versa.

6

Overcoming Information-Related Chaos

*The next best thing to knowing something
is knowing where to find it.*

—SAMUEL JOHNSON

*T*hree key problems can lead to information-related chaos:

♦ *Misplacement,* primarily caused by lack of effective systems and procedures; secondarily caused by carelessness and/or forgetfulness (linked to memory issues).

♦ *Misinformation,* primarily caused by gaps, inaccuracies, and inattention (linked to communication and time issues).

♦ *Miscomprehension,* caused by a broad range of information-processing impediments, including undiagnosed learning disabilities and dyslexia, language differences and difficulties, and exhaustion from overwork and/or lack of sleep.

My extensive experiences in the Land of Chaos have led me to conclude the following:

1. Misplacement of paper-based materials creates a disproportionate amount of information-related chaos.

2. Effective systems and procedures can prevent or greatly reduce misplacement and therefore counteract information-based chaos.

3. Well-designed information management systems counteract chaos by making it easy for people to find what they need, when they need it, without stress—and also making it easy for them to put things back.

Therefore, this chapter will focus, first and foremost, on how to establish and maintain effective systems and procedures for counteracting the misplacement of paper-based information. Suggestions for managing misinformation and miscomprehension will be discussed at the end of the chapter.

Drowning in Paper

Although electronic-based information presents various challenges, the fact remains that it's generally much easier to sort and organize computer files than paper ones. A mouse click or a keystroke can sort e-mail, for example, by date, subject, sender or message. Just try to do that with your piles of paper correspondence and faxes.

When people can't quickly locate documents that they or others need, chaos often ensues. The initial problem may create a ripple effect as more and more people are affected by the misplaced materials. Perhaps because it is so visible, paper-based information appears to provide people with more perceived chaos stress than its electronic counterparts. Oh, sure, people feel overwhelmed by Internet-generated info and excessive e-mail, but I hear more complaints about paper clutter than anything else. Over my many years as an organizing consultant, the majority of my clients and attendees at my seminars have told me that paper is their number one problem. They describe themselves as "drowning" in the tide of paper-based information that endlessly engulfs their workplaces; they

Just the Fax

According to a study by Boston-based Business Information Systems, in 1996 an estimated 35 billion sheets of office paper were used in fax machines alone. Placed end to end, those fax papers would circle the earth 241 times.

tell me it feels like they're wasting years looking for misplaced paper-work. (Of course, they're exaggerating—slightly. According to the Harper's Index, the average amount of time the average American spends looking for misplaced things over the course of a lifetime is merely one year.)

For the most part, the very machines that were supposed to eliminate paper have only added to the problem. The long-promised "paperless office" has proved to be as elusive as the fabled unicorn. Computers and faxes just generate more and more paper. (Even e-mail adds to the paper tide because so many people end up printing out e-mail messages—especially joke lists.) In fact, some people have discovered that computers are actually quite useful as sturdy pedestals on which they can stack plenty of paper.

A Case of Cubicle Chaos

Ironically, I've noticed that "computer people" often have the most paper—and the most problems with it. I'm reminded of Richard and Andrew, two computer programmers who had to share a work cubicle. They were like the Odd Couple. Andrew was organized and orderly, while Richard was a true Chaos Colleague, extremely disorganized and untidy to boot.

At first Richard made an effort to at least keep his paper clutter to himself. But over time, his piles began to migrate into Andrew's work space. Worse, because Richard could rarely locate documents or manuals when he needed them, he took to "borrowing" Andrew's easier-to-find materials. Then, invariably, he'd neglect to put them back—a habit that drove Andrew crazy.

These mismatched cubicle mates almost came to blows one day when Andrew stumbled over a pile of files that Richard had carelessly placed just inside the doorway in the path to Andrew's desk. The neatly collated stack of unnumbered pages Andrew was carrying flew all over the cubicle.

Miles of Piles

Richard could be a poster child for the Paperosis Misplacea Foundation. (Be sure to catch their upcoming fundraising telethon.) Paperosis

The Five Types of Piles

Piles of paper, if left alone, will breed at an alarming rate. According to my research, there are actually five types of piles.

1. *The Growing Pile:* It keeps getting higher and higher (especially if the mail isn't processed daily or if someone subscribes to numerous publications).
2. *The Stagnating Pile:* This used to be a Growing Pile until its growth was abruptly stunted, generally when it was hastily shoved into a bag, box, drawer, closet, or cabinet because someone was stopping by your office.
3. *The Diminishing Pile:* This is the pile that shows progress; it's getting smaller because someone is actually dealing with it instead of adding to it or hiding it away.
4. *The Distilled Pile:* This pile has gone through the previous three stages only to grind to a halt when its contents have been sifted down to sediment—the last few hard pieces of paper that seem impervious to the decision-making process. These are the papers that get shuffled and reshuffled endlessly because you feel as though you "can't decide" what to do with them—and you're never ready to just toss them out.
5. *The Double-Distilled Pile:* This occurs when there are several little Distilled Piles lying around and—in some pathetic, misguided effort to "clean up"—you sweep them all together and create one monstrous pile that seems completely impenetrable because you've already reshuffled the contents thousands of times and are no closer to making a decision than you were at the outset.

misplacea, in case you hadn't heard, is a chronic condition evidenced by the visible manifestation of information-related chaos; or, to put it in layperson's terms, piles and piles of paper.

Not that there's necessarily anything wrong with having piles of paper per se. It just depends on whether they are piles with purpose or pointless piles. If the piles have a purpose—that is, the "pilee" (or Pile Pilot) knows exactly what's in them and has them in a specific place for a specific reason—then there may not be a problem. (Mess Mavens, for example, tend to have piles with purpose.) But if the piles in question are actually pointless piles, then that's another story.

Pointless piles are often piles of postponed decisions. By now, most people have discovered that it's pretty unrealistic to try to practice that old rule of "handle a piece of paper only once." (What does that mean—once a day?) I think a more effective goal is to make a decision about each piece of paper the first time you handle it. If it's a paper you want to keep, decide where you'll want to put it (preferably not back in a pile) and then mark that decision in one corner of the paper (either on the document itself or on a Post-it note on the document). This way, the next time you *handle* it, you'll be able to really handle it—or at least you'll know what needs to be done with it.

If decision-making, or lack of it, is at the root of the Paperosis problem, here's a helpful remedy. The following exercise (which is based on

---

The Five W's of Clutter Control

When confronting a potential piece of paper clutter, always ask aloud:

1. **What** is this?
2. **Why** would I want to keep it?
3. **When** would I ever need it?
4. **Where** would I look for it?
5. **Who** else might have it?

This is a focusing exercise—asking the questions aloud forces you to focus instead of letting your mind go off on tangents unrelated to the paper in hand. What you're looking for is a specific answer to just one of the questions. I've found that at least 50 percent of the time, asking the first W is enough to cause you to throw out the piece of paper. The other 50 percent of the time, one of the other W's will help you decide whether the paper should be filed, acted on, or passed along to someone else.

the Journalists' Rule described in Chapter 5) is designed to facilitate the decision-making process. It will help any Pile Pilot make a decision fairly quickly instead of starting or adding to a pile.

Preventing Paperosis

Decision-making problems aren't the only cause of Paperosis. At least three other dilemmas contribute to it:

1. *Which papers do I have to keep?* There are two main types of paper document: records and resources. Records are finite in quantity (even though sometimes that may not seem apparent), while resources are infinite, thanks to the Information Age and the Internet. Therefore, the old rule "When in doubt, throw it out" applies mainly to resources: you can safely dump resource materials, for example, old trade journals and seminar handouts you'll probably never look at. But when it comes to financial and legal documents, records of your accomplishments, etc., the opposite rule applies: When in doubt, don't throw it out.

2. *How long must I keep them?* Different industries have different record-keeping requirements. Find out whether your company has any type of records retention schedule or guidelines; if it doesn't, you might want to see about setting up a records retention program. File purges should be scheduled at least annually to help keep Paperosis problems to a minimum. Old records can be stored in file storage boxes either on- or off-site. (For information on record-keeping requirements and records retention guidelines, contact the Association of Records Managers and Administrators—ARMA International—at 800-422-2762; www.arma.org.)

3. *Where and how should I keep them?* It's important to have delegatable paperwork systems and maintenance procedures. If your filing system is frustrating to use and your paper-flow procedures are nonexistent, it's not only difficult for you to maintain order, it's also hard for anyone else to help you. (And it's practically impossible for others to locate materials they may need from you when you're not available.) When creating any system, keep in mind that the most effective ones have three key attributes: they are simple, flexible, and growth-oriented.

Color Coding Cuts Chaos

One of the most effective tricks for simplifying systems is color coding. If you've ever watched a small child categorize objects by color, you know color coding can be wonderfully simple. Color-coded filing systems, diskette labels, and card-file systems (such as Rolodex) are all options worth exploring to help you or your chaos-creating colleague function better. And if your office uses a popular graphical interface system such as Windows or Macintosh, you can even color-code the computer files.

Reorganizing a Chaotic Filing System

Whether the task is to set up a filing system to combat your own chaos or that of someone you work with, anyone involved needs to have a

◈ ◈ ◈ ◈ ◈ *Watch-Out Window* ◈ ◈ ◈ ◈ ◈

When setting up systems with or for another Chaos Creator, many would-be organizers have a tendency to take charge so completely that they forget to solicit input from the person who theoretically will be using the system. People are always telling me about how they set up "this great system" for someone who never uses it. Invariably, I find out it's because the person setting up the system made no attempt to find out how the future system user thinks.

WATCH OUT! It's generally unwise to make assumptions about how someone else thinks or feels, even if you're sure you know them quite well. For example, avoid choosing colors for them—always ask if they have preferences or dislikes. Some people feel very strongly about certain colors (I've noticed that many of my clients seem to dislike orange, for example), while others may claim they really don't care. But most people have a favorite color or colors; the simple act of asking them what they like may open surprising doors.

basic understanding of the process. But when certain Chaos Creators are involved, watch out for communication-related chaos. For example, you may start to explain why the filing system needs reorganizing . . . but they end up hearing that what's needed is a new file cabinet (which also may be true, but only serves to complicate the issue further). Anyone intent on overcoming information-related chaos must comprehend the difference between a bunch of files and a filing *system*—that orderly underlying framework which provides a specific place for each file. Without this comprehension, chaos is inevitable.

When I see that look of uncomprehension on a client's face, I offer this image to contemplate: Think of each file as a piece of a jigsaw puzzle. It's much easier to know where to put the pieces when there's a picture to work from. Without the structure or pattern provided by the picture (the system), all you have is a jumble of pieces (the files).

Setting up or reorganizing a filing system is a task that often gets relegated permanently to back-burner status by File-o-phobes, which is what I call those who consistently show a fear of filing. For them, filing is an important-but-not-urgent sub-priority that gets put off until it reaches crisis proportions.

One of the major reasons many people dread redoing their filing system is because they don't know how to do it in a way that minimizes the mess and discomfort associated with the process. (Sounds like I'm discussing a nasty medical procedure, doesn't it?!) You may think it involves pulling out lots of files and dumping them on the floor, creating more chaos and confusion and causing business to grind to a halt. Well, it doesn't have to be that way.

When to Get Special Help

If you're dealing with a major filing system overhaul involving more system users and records (especially medical, legal, and financial), you've got a much bigger job ahead of you than the one outlined in the following pages. Unless you know all about stuff like records retention guidelines and records management programs, it would be wise to get professional assistance.

There are consultants who are experts in the field of records management—accredited ones, too (certified records managers, or CRMs). ARMA International (referred to earlier in this chapter) has a directory of consultants in this specialized field, plus over 200 publications relating to the topic.

I've created or restructured literally hundreds of filing systems for my clients over the past two decades. Along the way I've developed and refined a process that enables anyone to reorganize their files in an efficient and hassle-free manner.

My method is relatively simple. It doesn't create a mess. Business can continue uninterrupted; in fact, you can stop at any point during the process and not create confusion or impede progress. Of course, it isn't entirely painless—it does involve making decisions and thinking clearly, and there's no getting around the fact that it takes time.

Coordinating the Chaos-Conquering Process

If you're going to be leading the attack against information-related chaos, it's often important to involve others in the filing system reorganization process instead of doing it by yourself. That's because:

1. Their input is valuable; it gives you a better understanding of how they think. This is crucial to setting up a system that more than just one person will know how to use (or at least less likely to have an excuse not to use it).
2. Their involvement makes them familiar with the system and therefore more likely to actually use it.
3. The process can be easier to complete with two people working together. (Unless, of course, both of you are extremely disorganized and/or overwhelmed, in which case I'd recommend—if at all possible—either enlisting the aid of an organized associate or intern, or hiring an experienced professional organizer.)

Although you may be capable of doing it yourself, I've found that filing system reorganization usually goes faster—and is less tedious—when two compatible people work as a team.

But First . . . Don't Get Hung Up on Hanging Files

Over the years, I've lost count of how many people have said to me, "I hate hanging files! Don't try to get me to use them!" (Perhaps it is merely coincidental that these are the people who tend to have file drawers packed with a substance I refer to as "manila strudel": quasi-vertical layers upon layers of crumbling, flaky folders overstuffed with a variety of fillings.)

I'm not sure why some people have such a strong antipathy toward hanging files, but if you feel this way, I have three words of advice: Get Over It. This isn't just about files—it's about change. If something isn't working that well for you, why cling to it so fiercely? *Chaos Conquerors understand the importance of exploring alternative options. Do you?*

Manila Strudel, Anyone?

One excuse people make to justify using only manila folders is that you can fit more in a drawer if you don't use them with hanging files. To which I respond: Unless you've developed a taste for "manila strudel," squeezing more folders into a drawer is not going to make your life easier. Hanging files and expandable pockets may take up a little more drawer space, but when used properly they increase accessibility to your files. I consider it a worthwhile tradeoff.

For example, another option worth considering is expandable file pockets (undivided accordion files). These sit on the drawer bottom; unlike folders, they have good posture—no slumping. ("Folders" refers to either manila or colored interior file folders, tabbed third-cut or fifth-cut.) One key reason I recommend both hanging files and expandable file pockets is that both are designed to hold multiple folders. This feature allows you to group related folders together, which helps you categorize.

See, you don't have to abandon your beloved manila folders after all—just give them a better home.

Planning and Doing

Whether you're doing this for yourself or others, there are two main parts to the process: planning and doing. Each part has five steps.

"Planning" basically involves taking stock of the existing system and restructuring it on paper to create a "blueprint" of the new system.

"Doing" consists of the clerical work—relabeling old files or labeling new ones, color coding, and transferring contents.

Planning is the part that often makes Chaos Creators uncomfortable, because they may be unaccustomed to the planning process in general. They tend to want to jump right in and start moving things around so they feel like they're actually doing something, even if what they're really doing is making a bigger mess. It's like running in circles—they may not be getting anywhere, but at least they feel like they're moving.

Trying to make Chaos Creators understand the importance of planning can be frustrating. After all, they may have somehow managed to live a lifetime without planning. But they've got to get it sometime. I've found that sharing the following analogy is often an effective breakthrough tactic:

If you were going to build a house, would you go out and buy a bunch of bricks and lumber and roofing materials, dump them on the site, and then start hammering and drilling and digging around? Probably not. Not only would that be expensive and time-consuming, it would also be extremely ineffective.

Yet here's what many people do when they set out to organize or reorganize a filing system: They buy a bunch of folders and maybe even a new file cabinet, and then they start digging around in their files and papers until they get discouraged and give up.

So what's a better way? When building a house, a set of plans—a blueprint—is prepared before you start building. The same process applies when you're building (or reorganizing) a filing system: draw up your plans first. This type of blueprint is called a file index.

Once you've laid the groundwork for the planning step, you can get started. Here's a detailed description of my two-part process for planning and doing so you'll know exactly how to proceed. Don't worry—as with most instructions, participating in the actual process is simpler than reading about it.

How to Reorganize a Chaos Creator's Filing System (Yours or Someone Else's)

PART I: PLANNING

This process really needs to be a team effort, regardless of whose chaos is the source of the problem. So if you're taking any Chaos Creators

◆◆

A Word about Weeding

The approach I use favors weeding out the contents of the files after the system has been restructured. I've found that if you attempt to weed first, you'll come across various papers that aren't in the right files because the right files don't exist yet. Then you end up making little piles with them. If you first reorganize the system and then weed it, you're more likely to have a place for everything.

◆◆

under your wing, make sure they are there with you. On the other hand, if it's your chaos that's the problem, recruit or hire someone who will help keep you focused as you make your way through the forest of files.

Planning | Step 1. Block Out Time

Set aside a block of two to four hours of uninterrupted time. Unless your workplace situation is a rare oasis of calm during the work week, you'll probably need to come in on a weekend or even a holiday. (A hassle, true, but the long-term results will be worth it.)

Be sure to arrange a way to limit distractions such as telephone calls and visitors. Set up a work-friendly environment—comfortable temperature and seating, good lighting—and make sure your chaos-conquering team is prepared for the long haul, with snacks, beverages, and bathroom facilities available.

Planning | Step 2. List File Names

Having a list of current file names, or file index, makes the reorganizing process much simpler. A file index helps you see the big picture by giving you an effective way of viewing all your file names together (much easier than having to open drawer after drawer stuffed with folders). Because a file index lets you see at a glance exactly which files are already in place, it also makes it easier to figure out how to expand the system when files need to be added, reducing potential redundancies. A file index is also a great memory jogger for anyone who has trouble remembering file names and/or categories. *Bonus:* If you want to be able to delegate filing tasks, a file index will save you time when training others to use the system.

To create a file index, start by deciding where you want to begin—choose whichever file drawer or box seems like a good starting point. Then read off (or have your coworker read off), one by one, the name of each existing hanging file and/or nonhanging folder in the exact order—or disorder—that they're currently in. The file names should be written on a ruled pad or keyed into a computer (whichever is most handy) as they are called out. Ideally, one person does the reading and the other makes the list.

During this stage, redundancies often surface—multiple files that you or your colleagues recognize as having the same purpose despite their different labels. For example, in the home office of one of my clients there were six separate files (spread out among three file cabinets) for his automotive records, even though he only had one car. The files were labeled Automobiles, Car Info, Driving, Expenses/Cars, Volvo, and Tires. Every time he had the urge to file some car-related paperwork, he'd have trouble finding the right file and often ended up creating yet another one. This was a classic case of Redundant File Syndrome (RFS).

Like my car-crazed client, there are many victims of RFS. When symptoms of RFS are discovered during the listing process, I recommend combining the contents of the redundant files into one file. If there's too much paper, just group the files together and relabel only the first file in the group. This will make it easier for you later when you're physically setting up the new files.

Planning   Step 3. Evaluate

As you read aloud or record each file name, ask: "Is that a good name for this file?" If the answer is yes (and you agree), go on to the next file. But if the answer is no, or there's a pause, stop and ask: "What would be a better name for it?" You may need to suggest one; try to come up with a fairly broad heading that will be expansive enough to include more than one kind of paper, if possible. Not too broad a

❖ ❖ ❖ ❖ ❖ *Watch-Out Window* ❖ ❖ ❖ ❖ ❖

Since Chaos Creators are often unaccustomed to the planning process, they have a tendency to get antsy around this point and may want to take action by stopping to relabel the actual file instead of noting it on the list. A common play is to wheedle something like, "What about the do-it-now principle?" You'll be tempted to give in.

WATCH OUT! This is just a cleverly disguised version of Sidetracking. If you interrupt the planning process every time you or someone else wants to stop and "do" something—even if it is a potentially useful task—it will take a long, long time to finish the plan.

Instead, remember that (1) planning is a form of "doing it now"; and (2) repeatedly stopping and starting will derail the momentum and create the "two steps forward, one step back" syndrome. Keep in mind that there will be plenty of time for relabeling files during Part II. Finally, if all else fails, treat yourself and your partner to a snack. You deserve it.

heading though—one of my clients made that mistake by naming a category "Miscellaneous, Etc." (*Note:* Avoid spending more than half a minute discussing the options; otherwise it could take forever to finish this step.)

In some cases, one of you may not remember what the file is for. This generally happens either when the label is particularly ambiguous or the file is very old. One of you will then need to take a quick peek inside the file to evaluate the contents. *Caution:* Don't get sidetracked! Try not to read or weed the file—just scan the contents to get an idea of what's in there; 20 to 30 seconds should be sufficient. An exception: If you see something that's instantly recognizable as "toss-able"—such as outdated or irrelevant papers—throw it out. Make sure to have a wastebasket handy for these rare but happy occasions.

Once a better file name has been chosen, mark it next to the current file name on the list and circle it so that when it's time to relabel the files, you'll know which labels need to be created.

Files containing inactive but potentially important materials (such as old financial or legal records) should be margin-noted as Archival and put in marked storage boxes.

Planning   Step 4. Categorize

Whether the files are just an alphabetized, uncategorized mass or an un-alphabetized, uncategorized mess, now is the time to consider categorizing.

Some people initially have difficulty with the concept of categorizing. The idea of grouping like things or tasks together may be foreign to them. (A client once asked me, "What is a like thing?" It's one of those trick questions, like when a child asks you the meaning of "the opposite sex.") As with the concept of planning, I've found that using an analogy can help pierce the fog:

Think about how supermarkets and department stores are set up—products are grouped together based on similarity. Now think about how long it would take you to shop if all the merchandise was alphabetized instead of categorized!

Understand that categorizing cuts down on the number of files to skim through. This, in turn, reduces the amount of time it takes to find something. Note that a categorized filing system is *also* alphabetized, within the categories, a notion that may initially elude the uninformed.

I've found that once people comprehend that categorizing will save them time and make it easier to locate papers, they are less resistant to the concept of change, at least in this area.

Note: When you have relatively few files (say, under 25), it may be simpler just to label them clearly and put them in alphabetical order. But if you've got at least one drawer crammed with dozens of overstuffed folders, there's a good chance that categorizing will help produce order. If the system is already categorized, it's wise to reevaluate the existing categories to see if they need to be altered or added to.

When categorizing a filing system, it usually works best to use a limited number of broad categories. (I know a client hasn't quite gotten the concept when he says, "We're going to need *dozens* of categories!") In the majority of systems I've set up for clients, four or five major categories is average. (A very few have required as many as 10 categories.) But in some cases I've found that only two or three categories are needed: for example, General and Financial; or General, Clients, and Vendors. Basically you're only grouping batches of at least six files that seem to belong together. It's especially important for you and your coworkers to discuss which files go together. Be sure to make decisions *with* them, not *for* them.

Once you've completed Steps 2 and 3, you should have some sense of how, or if, the files can be grouped logically. The sample list of generic business file categories below might start you thinking.

File Fitness Formula

Three points to keep in mind for both computer and paper file fitness:

♦ Grouping files into categories makes it easier to quickly find what you're looking for.

♦ The files you use most often should be most accessible and easily identifiable.

♦ Weeding file contents regularly (also discarding or archiving inactive files) helps keep the systems working smoothly.

Sample Business File Categories

Category names are capitalized and underlined. Indented capitalized names are examples of the types of hanging files that might be found within these categories. Indented noncapitalized names indicate folders that go inside the hanging files. For example:

<u>CATEGORY NAME</u>
    HANGING FILE
        Interior Folder

<u>ARCHIVAL</u> (old files to put in storage)

<u>CLIENTS</u>
    (A–Z)

CORRESPONDENCE
   INCOMING
   OUTGOING
   NAMES (individual)

FINANCIAL
   EXPENSES/PETTY CASH
   PAYABLES
   RECEIVABLES

FORMS
   APPLICATIONS
   REQUISITIONS

GENERAL OFFICE ADMINISTRATION
   EQUIPMENT INSTRUCTIONS
      Fax
      Phone System
      Photocopier
   POLICIES/PROCEDURES
   STAFF RECORDS

REFERENCE/RESOURCES

VENDORS/SUPPLIERS/CONSULTANTS
   OFFICE PRODUCTS
   ORGANIZING CONSULTANTS
      Miracle Worker, The (Harriet Schechter)

The actual categorizing process works like this: First, make a list of potential file categories, using your list of existing files as a guideline. Or look over the Sample Business File Categories and see if any of them strike both you and your coworker as relevant to the system you're developing.

Next, read aloud each file name, one by one, from your file index and have your coworker respond to each with a category name that seems like a good match. For example, you might call out "Staff Records," and someone might respond with "Administration." Of course, some matching may be more difficult than other matching. Try to work as a team as much as possible; avoid the urge to control or influence anyone's responses. If someone seems stuck at any point, however, go ahead and suggest an option or two, but don't let yourself get dragged into a prolonged discussion. It's important to keep moving at a reasonably rapid pace before anyone collapses or your patience gives out.

Once you've agreed on a category, jot it in the margin next to the file name. Then move on to the next file name, until each file on the list has been categorized.

If this step sounds time-consuming, that's because it *is*—at first, anyway. But I've found that it speeds up as you move down the list and everyone involved becomes more comfortable with the categorizing process. Perhaps the most valuable part of this exercise is that each of you is becoming familiar with the system from the inside out. This is crucial to the goal of getting people to use the system.

After you've finished categorizing the list together, count up how many files you'll have in each category. There may be some surprises; for example, there may only be two files that belong in the Forms category once the redundant or outdated Forms files have been consolidated or eliminated. Decide whether (1) there's a need for more files in this category but they haven't been set up yet, or (2) this category isn't really necessary—the two files can be absorbed into the General category. Then change your list of categories if necessary.

When you've completed this step, you'll know the exact number of files for each category, at least up to this point. Possibly more files will be added or changed over time, but these will do for now. If you decide to replace your old files with new ones (see Step 5), you'll have a good idea how many you're going to need.

| Planning | Step 5. Color-Code |

This step involves two processes: deciding which colors to use, and obtaining the filing supplies to use in the "Doing" stage.

Although color coding the filing categories isn't necessary for every system, I've found that it's extremely effective for many situations. When it's kept simple, it can really work wonders for all types of Chaos Creators—and for the people who work with them, too. Of course, like anything else, there are both advantages and disadvantages to having a color-coded filing system:

Advantages include . . .

- Substantially reduced misfiling. According to Esselte-Pendaflex, color-coded filing systems reduce misfiling by approximately 50 percent.

- Simplified file labels. The number of words needed to identify files is reduced.

- Visual appeal. Attractive colors can make files seem more inviting to use.

Disadvantages include . . .

- Higher cost of files.

- Increased inventory (need to keep extra files and tabs on hand in different colors).

- Potential confusion. If too many colors are used, it can become confusing and counterproductive.

If you choose not to color-code, you can skip this step, but you'll be increasing the amount of time you spend creating file labels. Why? Because in a standard categorized (not color-coded) system, each file tab (label) usually contains both the category name and the file name; for example, FINANCIAL: Expenses, FINANCIAL: Payables, FINAN-CIAL: Receivables.

In a color-coded system, a color represents a category (e.g., green for Financial), thereby eliminating the need to crowd the category name onto the file tab. The labels become more effective because with fewer repetitive words on them, they're easier to read, and you can use larger lettering. (*Note:* For extra clarity, the first file in each category can be tabbed with a special label indicating the category name, as described below.)

Once the decision has been made to color-code the files, go back through your file index and assign one color to each category. Then count up how many files you'll need in each color, so you'll know exactly what file supplies to obtain. Currently, hanging files and matching interior folders are available in at least 10 colors. (File folders are even available with colorful patterns and illustrations on the outside, but I think of these as novelty items and generally don't recommend them for business use.)

Hanging files usually come with 2-inch-wide plastic label holders, or tabs, which are either clear or colored, depending on the type of file they come with. (These tabs are also sold separately.) I also recommend getting some 3-inch-wide tabs to use for the category name labels. Attach these larger tabs to the *center of the first file in each category*. This will enable anyone—even a memory-challenged Chaos Creator—to see at a glance which category each color represents.

Although I think the most effective way to color-code your filing system is with colored files, it's possible to do it by using just the colored tabs. This option costs less because you can use your existing hanging files (assuming they're all the same color and in fairly good condition) with the addition of the colored tabs, which come in packages of 25 and are quite inexpensive. However, if your files are disintegrating, you may as well go ahead and replace them with new, colorful files; they're really not that much more expensive than the old olive-drab kind. (I tried to point this out to one of my Chaos Creator clients, but he still insisted on stapling together his decrepit old files that were literally falling apart—a habit that drove his secretary crazy. Curiously, he was a millionaire who was paying my fee of $100 per hour without complaint. Go figure.)

You've now completed hours of planning, thinking things through, and making decisions. Give yourselves a pat on the back for getting this far along in the process. It's time for a break—you've earned it. You'll also need to obtain supplies before continuing on to the next part. Depending on whether this involves a trip down the hall to the supply room or a shopping expedition, you may need to schedule another day to complete the process. When you do begin the rest of the process, check out the checklist of filing supplies and be sure you have everything you need on hand to avoid any delays.

Technically, Part II of the process can be delegated to someone else (preferably not a Chaos Creator), providing your file index is clear enough for that person to follow. If you do delegate, I recommend you be on hand to at least supervise the following steps. And if you're the actual Chaos Creator, it's best to have your organized helper there.

Except for Step 5 (Weeding), your chaos-creating coworkers needn't be involved in Part II either, unless they are especially eager to be; in fact, it might go faster without them. Use your judgment. When I'm reorganizing a client's filing system, I often set up his or her new files off-

◈ ◈ ◈ ◈ ◈ *Watch-Out Window* ◈ ◈ ◈ ◈ ◈

Some Chaos Creators are skilled at throwing you off balance with their sanity-defying habits and enervating eccentricities. Without you realizing it, they can cunningly engage you in a fruitless discussion or pointless argument; meanwhile the minutes tick by until . . . "BZZZZZT! Time's up! Guess we won't be able to finish this today."

WATCH OUT! It's yet another Sidetracking gambit, masquerading as honest weirdness. Don't let yourself get sucked into this trap; it's often better to "go with the flow" instead of spending valuable time trying to lead a Chaos Creator to the trough of common sense, since they're not gonna drink from it anyway. From working with many Chaos Creators, I've learned how to quickly evaluate the relative importance of any given quirk and deal with it accordingly. In the case of the file-o-phobic millionaire, I refused to take the bait: After pleasantly recommending that he replace his battered files instead of repairing them, I moved on to the next task. (My motto: I hate exercise, especially an exercise in futility.) This aikido-like tactic causes the Chaos Creator's own resistance to work against them, often rendering them remarkably quiescent. Remember, you are the Chaos Conqueror. Your objective is to keep moving forward so this project gets completed before you retire or keel over. Don't waste time fighting silly skirmishes—just win the war!

site (at my office), using the file index; then I return the following week with the newly labeled file folders. I've found that it saves a lot of time (and therefore saves the client money) because I can work twice as fast when I'm alone and I don't have to answer questions or supervise the client.

If you do work with any Chaos Creators during the next stages, your greatest challenge may be—as before—to keep them focused on doing things one step at a time. Remember, the concept of grouping like tasks together instead of doing things in a piecemeal fashion may be alien to them. Be patient, and make sure you stay focused yourself.

Checklist of Filing Supplies to Obtain

QTY.	DESCRIPTION	COLORS
_____	Hanging files	_____
_____	Hanging box files (for bulkier materials)	_____
_____	Interior folders (manila or different colors)	_____
_____	Adhesive labels	_____
_____	2-inch plastic tabs, clear or colored	_____
_____	3-inch plastic tabs, clear	_____
_____	File boxes or containers	_____
_____	File cabinet or storage unit with hanging file frames	_____

PART II: DOING

 Step 1. Create Labels

Before you actually sit down to create the new file labels, decide which labeling method to use. There are four.

Block printing (by hand). Good for filing systems of up to approximately 60 files. Labels should be legibly printed (all capitals). This is usually the easiest method for making and maintaining labels—they can be changed or added most quickly.

Computer-generated. If you used a computer while making the list of files and categorizing, you can get a program such as LabelPro for printing out the list on individual labels. Another option is a computer-labeling accessory like the Avery Personal Label Printer, which enables you to print labels in different sizes. Obtaining software that allows you to print out lettering directly onto the perforated cardboard tab inserts that come with hanging files may be more trouble and expense than it's worth. Instead, adhesive-backed labels are used which often must be trimmed or folded back to fit the tab inserts.

Typewriter. If you want to avoid the trimming and peeling process described above, don't have or want a label program, didn't use a computer for the blueprint, can't block-print worth a damn, and/or have dozens and dozens of files, then typing the labels is probably your best option. Since tab inserts come in perforated strips or sheets, you can type directly onto them.

Labeling machine. Both Kroy and Brother manufacture labeling machines that are as far removed from the old Dymo labelers as a horse and buggy is from a Ferrari. For well under $100 you can get what looks and functions like a mini-computer printer and produces elegant, easy-to-read, long-lasting adhesive-backed labels in a range of styles, sizes, and colors. I don't recommend this option for larger filing systems because it's fairly labor-intensive to have to key in the label names, print them out in small batches, cut them apart, peel off the adhesive backing, and then apply them to the tab inserts. However, if you already have a labeling machine and don't mind this process, go right ahead. Use black-on-white or black-on-clear, all caps, bold face lettering for best legibility.

Doing　　Step 2. Set Up Tabs

Once all the labels are printed, separate them and insert them into the plastic tabs, using the 2-inch tabs for file headings and 3-inch tabs for category headings. If you've decided to use different-colored files for color coding (as opposed to using only colored tabs), then you can use either the matching tabs that come with the files or clear tabs.

An advantage to using clear tabs is that they make the labels a bit easier to read, especially for anyone who doesn't have perfect vision. Some people find the darker tab colors—red and green in particular—more difficult to see through. I always show my clients what a label looks like inside the darker tabs so that they can decide whether they prefer the clear ones or not. You might want to do the same with anyone who'll be using the system regularly.

If colored tabs are to be used, be sure to put labels into tabs that match the color-coding specified in the file index.

Doing　　Step 3. Tab Files

After the tabs are finished, you're ready to set up the new files. It's helpful to have a file box or container handy to hold the files upright and in order as you get them tabbed. This box will also come in handy later when you're transferring file contents.

There are two burning questions people have about tab placement:

♦ Do you put them on the front or the back of the file?

♦ Do you stagger them or put them in rows?

First of all, the File Police aren't going to arrest you if you tab files "incorrectly," as long as they're tabbed consistently. That said, you should know that according to Pendaflex and other industry experts, tabs should go on the front of hanging files—the reverse of what's generally done with interior or manila folders. You can locate and open a file more quickly when it's tabbed on the front.

Regarding the second question, once again, either way can work fine, but I've found that staggering the file tabs does take more time, especially during this stage in the process. You can always go back and stagger them later if you prefer, but while you're setting up the new files, just line up the tabs in rows.

Put the 3-inch category tabs in the center of the first file in each category. Some people like to use a separate, empty file as a category divider, but invariably I find they end up sticking "miscellaneous" papers in there as time goes by. Use your judgment.

Once you've completed tabbing all the files, give yourselves a pat on the back! Step back together and admire the overall effect of these pristine, "virgin" files. If you've created a color-coded system with several categories, the rainbow effect can be quite appealing. Enjoy it now; like new carpeting, it won't look quite as fresh after it's had some use.

| Doing | Step 4. Transfer File Contents |

This is the easiest step of the entire process. All you have to do is transfer the contents of the old files into the new ones. Since there may be quite a few brand-new file names, be sure to consult your file index to avoid any potential confusion. If you followed the directions in Step 3, you should have no trouble figuring out which old file contents get transferred into which new file folder.

Designate an Archival file storage box to pack up any really old files, and mark the outside of the box to indicate the contents and, if possible, a "destroy date."

| Doing | Step 5. Weed Files

Weeding files is a maintenance task (remember the Maintenance Time Worksheet in Chapter 4?), and like most maintenance, when it's been sufficiently neglected it becomes a project—and a fairly unpleasant one at that.

Assuming the files are due for major liposuction, I recommend you set aside a separate block of uninterrupted time to work together on this project.

Speed Weeding

When I help clients weed their files, I train them to do it as quickly and effectively as possible. I call this process "Speed Weeding," and it works for both project and maintenance file weeding. The rules are:

♦ Stay focused. Remember, "Weeding, not reading."

♦ Keep moving forward. No going back in the trash to rescue anything (unless you've accidentally discarded money or legal documents).

When to Weed

People are always asking me, "How often should I weed my files?" There's no hard and fast rule—it depends on many variables. Some companies have records retention schedules and rules specifying when to weed, what to archive, etc.; others leave it up to the discretion of individual workers. There are people who swear by the "one file per day" weeding method (i.e., maintenance) and those who prefer annual file purges (i.e., projects). Still another option is the "In-Out Inventory Rule"—every time you go to file a paper, see if you can get rid of something else from that file.

Often I use a ticking timer, set for 15-minute increments, to set the pace and create a sense of urgency that deters dawdling. Speedy weeding is essential to getting through this process before you collapse.

If anyone gets stuck and can't seem to decide whether to keep, toss, or refile a piece of paper—a fairly common occurrence—try asking one or more of the following questions:

♦ Did you remember you had this before you looked at it just now?

♦ If you got rid of it, could you get it again—and would it be worth the trouble?

♦ If you keep it, will you know where to find it?

As with the listing and categorizing stages, having Chaos Creators participate in the weeding process is essential to their ultimate understanding of how the system works. Becoming intimately familiar with the reorganized filing system makes it more likely that they will actually use it instead of always calling on someone else to help unearth something from their piles or files.

Avoiding a Paper Hangover

Since weeding can be a rather grueling process, I recommend limiting it to a couple of hours at a stretch, unless you take periodic breaks. (Set the timer for 10 minutes maximum to limit break time.) Otherwise you'll run the risk of getting what I call a "paper hangover." That's when the mind begins to rebel after making too many paper-related decisions, and you start using poor judgment. If you keep working after the onset of a paper hangover, there's a tendency to make some unwise and ultimately regrettable decisions.

One of my clients, the owner of a small appliance repair shop, forgot to heed this advice. One day, in a frenzy of weeding while alone in her office, she succumbed to a massive paper hangover–induced urge to discard what she hazily recalled were several boxes of old client records. Later, as she was recovering with a tall frosty drink, the awful truth dawned on her that one of the boxes actually contained all of her employee records and other important documents (in a file labeled "Important Papers," no less). Fortunately the trash hadn't been picked up yet, so she was able to salvage the crucial files. But she learned a valuable lesson.

Subscribitis

While weeding, be ruthless in disposing of old magazines and journals that have been saved for no good reason. If your publication piles appear limitless, you may have a condition I call "Subscribitis," which is caused by subscribing to more publications than can be read in any one lifetime. I've found that people who suffer from Subscribitis often have a problem with "shoulds" (as in, "I really *should* read that . . . and that . . . and that") and "can'ts" (as in, "I *can't* get rid of that—I haven't read it yet").

Overcoming Subscribitis isn't easy. The process involves:

♦ Accepting the fact that it is impossible to read everything you think you "should" read. (Some people find it too painful to accept this and remain lifelong Subscribitis sufferers.)

♦ Reviewing your Maintenance Time Worksheet from Chapter 3 and estimating how much weekly "reading maintenance" time you can realistically afford to spend keeping up with your periodicals. (*Hint:* 168 hours may not be a realistic estimate.)

♦ Deciding on a manageable number of publications and editing your list of subscriptions accordingly. (*Tip:* I've observed that approximately one daily paper or bulletin plus one weekly newsletter plus two monthly journals seems to be the maximum manageable number for many people.)

Go with the Flow

No matter how effective a filing system is or how well it's maintained, there are always going to be some papers that don't seem to fit. For example, many people aren't comfortable filing away papers that relate to active projects. As one of my clients once put it, "Once it's filed away, I think it's done." Fear of "out of sight, out of mind" can create a tendency to pile active papers on any available horizontal surface.

That's why I recommend setting up a very visible paper-flow system. It gives you a way to keep your active papers out, yet organized, so that when you sit down to work you don't end up spending half your time treasure hunting. The great philosopher Winnie-the-Pooh must have been mulling the true purpose of paper-flow systems when he mused, "Organizing is what you do before you do it so that when you do it, it's not all mixed up."

The most basic form of paper-flow system consists of the classic in-out boxes, the butt of innumerable jokes. I've found that the in-out system is a bit too simplistic to work well for most people in general and for Chaos Creators in particular.

The first step to creating an effective paper-flow system is to identify the main categories of paper that flow through the work space. The second step is to label baskets or stacking trays with the category names. General paper-flow categories include Correspondence, Meetings, To Read, To File, Active Projects, and Calls; categories that are more project-specific may be necessary as well.

The trick to keeping a paper-flow system from getting clogged is to allocate sufficient time to maintain it—to keep moving the papers forward (i.e., "flow") instead of letting them stagnate. Yes, it always comes back to Maintenance Time, sooner or later; that's why I say life is 90 percent maintenance.

Miscomprehension and Misinformation

What if paper flow and filing aren't a problem, but chaos happens because you (or someone you work with) consistently have trouble comprehending, producing, or processing information accurately? Here's what I suggest.

First, identify the specifics of the problem(s). Consider whether the Chaos Creator in question . . . .

- ◆ Does not understand English sufficiently well.
- ◆ Has a learning disability or any other type of impairment that might interfere with comprehension or information processing.
- ◆ Appears either exhausted from overwork or sleep-deprived.

Labeling Mistakes to Avoid

I've found it's usually futile to designate a tray as "Urgent," "Hot," "Do or Die," or a similarly frantic-sounding label. Generally speaking, truly urgent paperwork will end up on your chair or heaped in the middle of your desk (possibly on top of an older pile). This is reality.

Other common mistakes that sabotage paper-flow systems include:

♦ Too many categories *or* too few categories

♦ Labels that aren't readable

♦ Containers too small to hold enough *or* too large

♦ Is suffering from a chronic health problem (physical or mental).

♦ Might have a problem with substance abuse.

♦ Could be in the wrong job or even the wrong career.

If you don't believe any of these possibilities apply to you or your chaos-creating coworker, see if you can think of other options. For example: Perhaps, upon reflection, the possibility occurs to you that the problem could relate to miscommunication (a potential precursor to misinformation). In that case, you might be able to utilize suggestions from Chapter 5.

If, however, you answered yes to at least one of the listed possibilities, then outside help is probably advisable. Recognizing your own predicament isn't easy. It's a big step to admit that you have a problem which could be both affecting your own work quality or output and also creating chaos for others. If you are ready, please get help. Life is short—don't let correctable chaos-causing impediments hold you back.

Certain workplaces and many communities have various social and health care services available that offer free or inexpensive assistance for almost any type of challenge. Not sure how to find the help you need? Be resourceful. You can always start by checking your local phone directory's Government Pages listings and doing a little research by phone.

If the problem, however, belongs to someone you work with, getting him or her to go for help presents a different type of challenge. Whether or not you are in a position of authority, you should proceed cautiously—and with tact. Chapter 8 will show you specific steps, tactics, and approaches for dealing effectively with this and other types of Chaos Creator challenges.

But first, there's one final chaos category left to explore: Projects.

7

Preventing Project-
Related Chaos

*The world is full of willing people—some willing
to work, the rest willing to let them.*

—Robert Frost

*P*rojects involve time, information, communication, and memory. This means that the potential for chaos in each of these categories expands when they are combined in a project. (Scary, isn't it?)

But wait—what exactly is a project?

Let's go back for a moment to the two types of time described in Chapter 3: Project Time and Maintenance Time. Maintenance Time, as I hope you'll recall, is the time spent on routine, never-ending tasks (processing mail, returning phone calls, filing). Project Time, on the other hand, is for more complex work. Projects are composed of multiple tasks. They also tend to have definable goals, budgets, a beginning-middle-end sequence, and deadlines. Especially deadlines. More on those in a moment.

Project management therefore includes something from each of the chaos cure categories—a case of the sum being greater than the total of its parts (or something like that). So any of the solutions described for the other categories may come in handy whether you're a project-puncturing Chaos Creator yourself or you have to work with one.

However, the following tools and tricks are included to help you with certain kinds of chaos not covered elsewhere in this book. *Note:* Project management is actually a bona fide field that is growing rapidly. It has its own lingo, its own organization (the Project Management Institute), its own high priests and priestesses—you get the idea.

The Story of a Chaos Colony

The eight people who made up the Creative Services Department at the A+ Advertising Agency were all highly creative. Unfortunately for Annette, their new boss, they were also extremely disorganized.

Each person had been hand-picked by Annette's predecessor, a man who was fairly chaotic himself yet who somehow had managed to keep his team on track. He had been popular and well-respected by his troops, and under his leadership this mildly dysfunctional group had managed to be productive and even create award-winning ad campaigns.

When he left and Annette took over, things began to fall apart. Although the team still came up with great ideas, their project follow-through was erratic and they couldn't seem to meet deadlines. Clients started complaining, upper management got nervous, and morale began to drop. Poor Annette felt as though she was dealing with a schizophrenic octopus, its eight tentacles at cross-purposes.

Projects, like people, come in all shapes and sizes and have many parts (which may flail around, as Annette discovered). Some projects involve teams of people like A+ Advertising's merry band of Chaos Creators, while in other cases just one person may be responsible for seeing a project through from beginning to end. But no matter what type of project you're facing, you can avoid project-related chaos by using the following techniques and tools.

Plan to Plan

Essential to successful project management are thorough planning and follow-through—the two areas most foreign to Chaos Creators. People who generate project-related chaos often appear to be particularly allergic to planning. And since 90 percent of a successful project is in the planning, this is where the problems start. Especially when a team is involved.

Effective project planning begins by including everyone who will be involved in the project. (The fewer people involved, the simpler it should be—theoretically, anyway.) If the people who are part of the project team are left out of the planning stage, the chances of meeting a deadline diminish. Without all the participants' input, you can't get a complete picture of what's involved and how long each step of the project should take.

Once you've assembled all the parties involved, it's crucial to plan completely, laying out all the steps from beginning to end, estimating what's involved in each step, including a time frame. Project management expert Sharon Kristensen Deméré, owner of the Menlo Park, California–based company Organization Plus,® suggests brainstorming sessions (it usually takes several) to accomplish this. When she helps clients with this planning stage of a project, she has them create a Project Map to identify each step.

Using the Project Map

The purpose of a Project Map is to diagram each aspect of what needs to be accomplished to successfully complete the project. Ideally, this diagramming process should be completed by the end of the brainstorming sessions. Here are the steps for using the Project Map:

1. After the person in authority gathers everyone around the meeting table, go to the inner circle on the form and write in the mission. *Example:* Mission: "Award-winning ad campaign for XYZ Co. product."
2. Fill in the time line space. *Example:* "Three months."
3. The team discusses the objectives and strategies, using the spokes (the lines radiating from the circle) to list them.
4. Fill in the Benefits/Rewards box. Then ask whether these justify the effort to be expended.
5. Prioritize steps (a, b, c or 1, 2, 3)
6. Use the Commitment Calendar on pages 146–47.

All of these process steps can be effective whether you're working alone on a project or with others. They can help you see the big picture and track how you're doing.

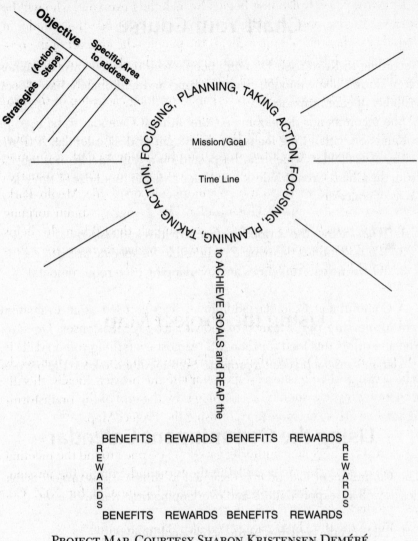

PROJECT MAP. COURTESY SHARON KRISTENSEN DEMÉRÉ,
© 1989 ORGANIZATION PLUS.®

After you've laid out all the various steps in the project, you'll need to take a look at the deadline you're aiming for and determine whether or not it's really feasible. Again, it's crucial to include all the project participants so you can get a realistic view of what the deadline should be.

Chart Your Course

According to Kristensen Deméré, people who routinely miss deadlines often do not allow enough planning time and additionally have "poor visibility of commitments."

She recommends developing a Commitment Calendar to be used in conjunction with a time management system or desk calendar. A Commitment Calendar, which can be posted on a wall (ideally, not too far from the Chaos Creator's desk), provides a visible reminder of three key areas of concern:

1. *What* (shows the various project activities and tasks)
2. *Who* (identifies the people responsible for specific tasks)
3. *When* (reveals time lines and overlapping time requirements)

A Commitment Calendar additionally can be used as an evaluation tool to measure performance of individuals, says Kristensen Deméré. She also offers this food for thought: "Almost everything you do daily is, in a larger sense, a piece of a project." So remember to keep the big picture in mind.

Using the Commitment Calendar

The Commitment Calendar is designed to show various project activities as well as responsibilities and overlapping time requirements.

1. List specific activities in the activity column.
2. On the first line, show total time required for the project by drawing a line from the start date to the desired completion of the project.
3. Fill in the Activity, Duration, Start, and Finish dates in the columns provided.
4. On the calendar side, plot in the start and finish for each activity and identify who is responsible for each activity.
5. Where appropriate, draw in linkage lines, linking one activity to another. Linkage lines indicate which activity is dependent on an-

other, for example, an activity that cannot begin until another linked activity is completed.

6. Use the area at the bottom of the calendar to specify the legend that you are using for the calendar. Symbols are used to represent activity duration, dependencies, and results. When using the calendar to evaluate project or individual results, the project leader can use symbols to show if deadlines were met, and if the deadlines were extended, the reason for the extension.

Commitment calendars can be formatted in numerous ways. When using project management software, different formats are built into programs. Ready-made forms are also available, or you can draw your own. Each column can represent one day in a month, a one- or two-week period, or even an entire month for a project that spans a year or more.

Turning a Chaos Colony into a Winning Team

Exactly how does this process work when you have a Chaos Colony on your hands like Annette did? Her challenge was to figure out how to get the Creative Services team to consistently follow through on projects and meet client deadlines. This is how she handled it.

Enlisting the help of a project management consultant, Annette established a workable process that enabled her team to stay on track without squelching its award-winning creative impulses. Here are the chaos-controlling steps they took which vastly improved her Chaos Colony's work flow:

First, Annette initiated weekly brainstorming sessions. Then she introduced the concept of mapping out a project, which became a key part of the sessions. Finally, she had the team create a giant Commitment Calendar (p. 146) for tracking all projects. Annette also made sure it was maintained. Ultimately, she was able to get her department running both on track and on time.

COMMITMENT CALENDAR™

ID	ℹ	Task Name	Duration	Start	Finish
1					
2					
3					
4					
5					
6					
7					
8					
9					
10					
11					
12					
13					
14					
15					
16					
17					
18					
19					

Project:

Date:

Project Start/End ○ • • • • • • • • ☆

Task Start/End

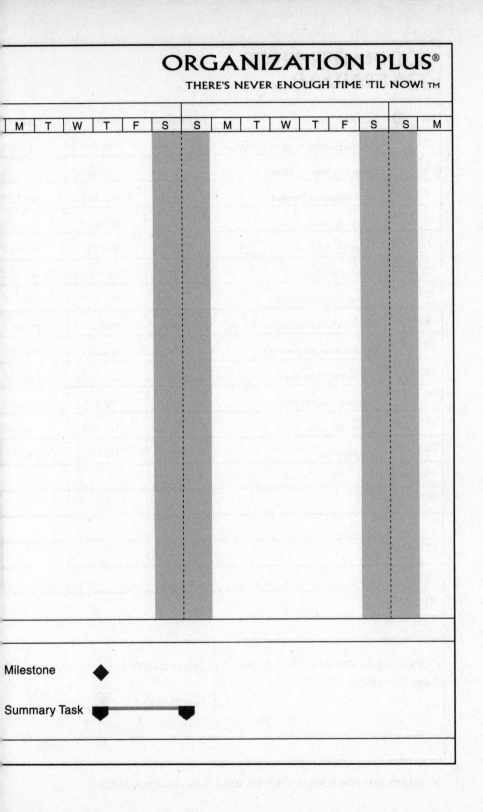

ORGANIZATION PLUS®

THERE'S NEVER ENOUGH TIME 'TIL NOW! ™

| M | T | W | T | F | S | S | M | T | W | T | F | S | S | M |

Milestone

Summary Task

COMMITMENT CALENDAR™

ID	ⓘ	Activity	Duration	Start	Finish
1	▦	Process Planning for an Ad Campaign	5 days	Fri 5/14	Thu 5/20
2	▦	Set-up Two Planning Mtgs.	1 hr	Fri 5/14	Fri 5/14
3		**Mtg.1 - Mapping Process**	**0.5 days**	**Mon 5/17**	**Mon 5/17**
4	▦	Identify Mission/Goal	1 hr	Mon 5/17	Mon 5/17
5	▦	Identify Time Line	30 mins	Mon 5/17	Mon 5/17
6	▦	Map Out Objectives	1.25 hrs	Mon 5/17	Mon 5/17
7	▦	Map Out Action Steps	1.25 hrs	Mon 5/17	Mon 5/17
8	▦	Review & Further Development of Map	2 days	Mon 5/17	Mon 5/17
9	▦	**Mtg. 2 - Complete Planning**	**0.38 days**	**Thu 5/20**	**Thu 5/20**
10		Prioritize Objectives	1 hr	Thu 5/20	Thu 5/20
11	▦	Assign Responsibility	30 mins	Thu 5/20	Thu 5/20
12	▦	Prioritize Action Steps	1 hr	Thu 5/20	Thu 5/20
13	▦	Review Plan	30 mins	Thu 5/20	Thu 5/20
14					
15					
16					
17					
18					
19					

Project: USING A "COMMITMENT CALENDAR ™"

Date: May 16–20

Project Start/End ◯ • • • • • • • • • ☆

Task Start/End ◤▬▬▬▬▬◢

ORGANIZATION PLUS®

THERE'S NEVER ENOUGH TIME 'til NOW! ™

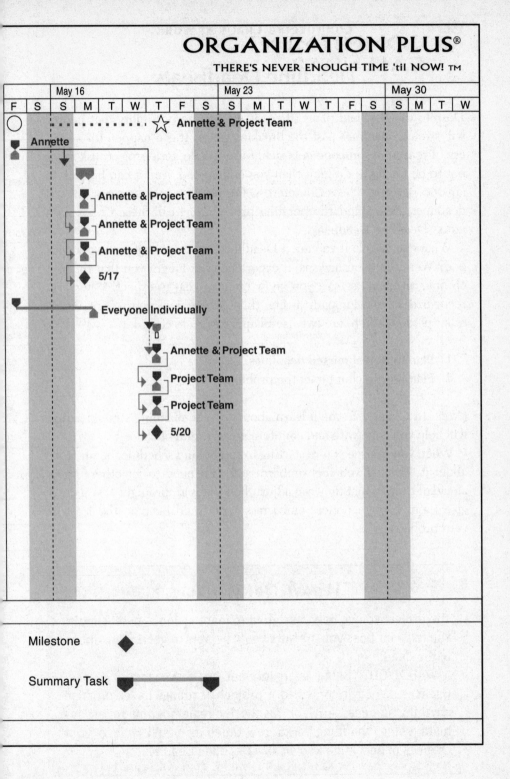

| | | May 16 | | | | | | | | May 23 | | | | | | | | May 30 | | | |
| F | S | S | M | T | W | T | F | S | S | M | T | W | T | F | S | S | M | T | W |

Annette & Project Team

Annette

Annette & Project Team

Annette & Project Team

Annette & Project Team

5/17

Everyone Individually

Annette & Project Team

Project Team

Project Team

5/20

Milestone

Summary Task

Deadline Deadbeats

Despite the best-laid plans, there is always the possibility that people will stretch deadlines past the breaking point. It can happen for a variety of reasons—someone gets sick, for example, or a project task turns out to be far more difficult than you anticipated. And it can happen to anyone—even to Chaos Conquerors. For some people, however, missed deadlines are a standard operating procedure. I call these Chaos Creators "Deadline Deadbeats."

What can you do if you are a Deadline Deadbeat or if you work with one? Well, the good news is, if experience has taught you that this is a chronic problem, at least you know by now what to expect. When you recognize a behavior pattern like this—whether in yourself or in another person—there are two useful approaches to consider:

1. Plan to expect missed deadlines.
2. Plan how to counteract the problem.

(*Note:* In Chapter 8, you'll learn about specific planning strategies that will help you cope with and counteract every kind of chaos.)

When you can see you're starting to run behind schedule, be up-front about it. Even if you feel embarrassed, you need to let others know ahead of time so that they can adjust their plans accordingly. If you don't give them enough notice, embarrassment could become the least of your problems.

❖ ❖ ❖ ❖ ❖ *Watch-Out Window* ❖ ❖ ❖ ❖ ❖

The project you've been assigned to manage looks fairly simple. You tell your boss you are sure you'll be able to get it done ahead of the deadline.

WATCH OUT! Being overconfident can have chaotic consequences. When it comes to a project deadline, never promise anything unnecessarily or rashly. By remembering to always build some "padding" into the timeline, you'll reduce your chances of becoming known as a Deadline Deadbeat.

If you work with someone who has a reputation for being a Deadline Deadbeat, your best bet is to always give them a false deadline with plenty of hidden padding—and never, ever let them know the real deadline. You may want to practice your acting skills so that when the time comes to act surprised, disappointed, and upset about the inevitable missed deadlines, you'll be able to put on a convincing performance.

Project Management Software

For anyone responsible for handling projects on a regular basis, project management software may be helpful. Although none of the many programs available are particularly user-friendly (Microsoft Project is said to be relatively simple, but the key word here is "relatively"), they still can be quite useful. That is, as long as everyone involved in the project has access to a computer.

Also, remember that the computer won't actually do the project any more than paper-flow trays will do the papers you stack in them. It won't even do all the planning. What it will do is create a time line for you after you enter information on all the various activities and parties involved. Ask your local software store what's available.

You'll find more ideas on how to deal with project-, time-, memory-, communication-, and information-related chaos problems in the chaos case studies described in Part III.

PART III

Conquering Chaos

OVERVIEW

*T*he chapters in this section will show you specific ways to assess your approach and prepare a plan for counteracting both your own chaos and, in particular, the chaos caused by others in your workplace.

In Chapter 8, you'll discover chaos-controlling strategies that can be adapted to any type of workplace situation. Two key forms are provided and demonstrated: The Chaos Log and the Focus Form. You'll learn how to facilitate positive change in others and yourself and what to do if a particular approach isn't working. And you'll find out how a Mess Maven was able to transform herself into a Chaos Conqueror. Expect to be informed and captivated.

Chapters 9 through 12 contain 16 real-life chaos case histories, with 48 use-it-now techniques for achieving both immediate and long-term solutions. Each of the four chapters addresses one type of Chaos Creator: The Deceptive Chaos Creator (DCC), the Creative Chaos Creator (CCC), the Oblivious Chaos Creator (OCC), and the Bureaucratic Chaos Creator (BCC). Expect to be entertained and educated.

Note: The following organizational chart is included to help you zero in on whichever type of workplace (there are 16 different kinds represented), working relationship (boss, assistant, coworker, client), and type of chaos (time-, memory-, communication-, information-, or project-related) may be of particular interest to you.

Case Histories Organizational Chart

CASE HISTORY	ROLE	WORKPLACE	CHAOS CREATOR/ CHAOS CONQUEROR	CHAOS CATEGORY	PAGE #
Chapter 9: Deceptive Chaos Creators					
1	Boss	Clothing Manufacturer	Norman / Ellen	Communication	183
2	Employee	Public Relations Agency	Rachel / Dana	Time and Communication	185
3	Coworker	Magazine Publisher	Dan / Brian	Project	188
4	Assistant	Condo Management Office	Jean / Erica	Information and Project	191
Chapter 10: Creative Chaos Creators					
5	Employee	Software Design Firm	Kevin / Terri	Information	198
6	Assistant	Executive Search Company	Nikki / Carla	Communication	201
7	Client	Bookkeeping Company	Ross / Ed	Project	203
8	Partner	Sporting Goods Wholesaler	Joe / Steve	Memory	207
Chapter 11: Oblivious Chaos Creators					
9	Client	Desktop Publishing Firm	Greg / Diane	Communication	213
10	Boss	Landscaping Business	Hal / Chris	Memory	217
11	Assistant	Insurance Company	Kim / Alan	Information	220
12	Partner	Real Estate Brokerage	Susan / Dennis	Time	223
Chapter 12: Bureaucratic Chaos Creators					
13	Boss	Nonprofit Organization	Julie / Lisa	Time and Information	228
14	Coworker	Government Agency	Sid / Maria	Project	230
15	Subordinate	Law Firm	Rita / Zack	Communication	233
16	Assistant	Retail Chain	Barry / Jim	Memory	235

8

When Organized Isn't Enough:

STRATEGIES FOR BECOMING A CHAOS CONQUEROR

To fail to plan is to plan to fail.
—BENJAMIN FRANKLIN

*T*he five preceding chapters have shown you how to become more organized. You've learned of tactics and tools for controlling your own chaos-causing habits and gotten tips for coping with some of the chaos created by others. Now you're about to find out how to go beyond organizing by *strategizing* so you'll be able to counteract any type of chaos caused by every type of Chaos Creator. At last—you're ready to enter the realm of the Chaos Conqueror!

Well, almost. First, you'll need to make just a couple of adjustments.

Choose Your Goal

It's time to decide whether this is a goal you'd like to set for yourself. Unless you're clear about the benefits of any new goal, it can be difficult to commit yourself to changing your behavior or learning a new set of skills. Therefore, the following table provides a shamelessly biased menu of benefits that aspiring Chaos Conquerors might hope to gain.

Also, you get to wear a nifty costume (see illustration on page 159), and not just on Halloween either. Plus, there's the official Chaos Conqueror badge, wand, and decoder ring you get when you send $19.95 to me at the address on the back of your box of cereal.

The Top 10 Reasons to Become a Chaos Conqueror

RESULTS = REDUCED:	IMPACT = INCREASED:	BENEFITS = IMPROVED:
Aggravation	Satisfaction	Outlook
Anger	Calm	Mood
Blood pressure	Well-being	Health
Fear	Power	Control
Frustration	Patience	Response
Rancor	Recognition	Reviews
Stress	Time	Productivity
Strife	Accord	Teamwork
Tension	Relaxation	Digestion
Weariness	Alertness	Sex life

Adjust Your Attitude

Once you've decided that, yes, you really do want to be a Chaos Conqueror—for your own sake and/or that of others—then your next step is to make a deliberate decision to adjust your attitude. (If you go back and review the Organized Person–Chaos Conqueror comparison on page 52 in Chapter 2, you'll notice that the key difference between a Chaos Conqueror and the typical organized person is attitude.)

Changing your attitude about anything is rarely easy. It often takes ongoing, conscious effort and commitment. You must decide whether the anticipated results are appealing enough to warrant the exertion involved. (Take another look at that table of benefits.)

To help you on your way, I created the Triple-A Attitude Adjustment Program to simplify the process of developing a Chaos Conqueror attitude. *Always:*

◆ *Assume* that you are more organized than anyone you work with in any capacity. (But act with tact—this is an internal assumption you're making.)

◆ *Anticipate* potential chaos-causing activity that others may perpetrate. Be thinking ahead at all times.

CHAOS CONQUEROR

- *Appreciate* (verbally or in writing) any effort made by Chaos Creators—and others—to curb their chaotic tendencies. As Dale Carnegie noted, "Three-fourths of the people you will ever meet are hungering and thirsting for appreciation. Give it to them and they will love you."

Here's why the Triple-A Attitude Adjustment Program works:

When you *assume* that others are less organized than you, you are ready to be pleasantly surprised if your assumption is wrong and forgivingly tolerant if it's right. You'll also armor yourself against disappointment, despair, and disgust—energy-draining emotions

that people often experience when they allow themselves to be vic-
timized by Chaos Creators.

When you *anticipate* chaos-induced crises, you empower yourself to
conquer chaos before it occurs—always the best way to avert
minor and major catastrophes. Anticipation leads to preparation,
and preparation leads to power.

When you actively *appreciate* others' efforts, you simultaneously dis-
arm and empower them—a great way to make them more receptive to your overt or covert guidance.

Assume, anticipate, appreciate—you might want to write those down
and post them on your bathroom mirror or in your planner to remind
yourself to practice your Chaos Conqueror attitude daily. Once it has
become second nature, you'll be more capable than ever of conquering
chaos at work.

But let's not get too cocky yet. True, attitude is important—but it's not
everything.

Chaos-Conquering Characteristics

Just as Chaos Creators have certain habits and characteristics, so too do
Chaos Conquerors. I've observed that Chaos Conquerors tend to consistently:

♦ Strive to take care of themselves physically and emotionally.

♦ Recognize that they always have a choice in how they can react to
any given situation or opportunity.

♦ Be capable of making quick decisions and then moving on.

♦ Be effective planners—focused yet flexible.

♦ Know how to create and utilize effective systems, and are always
on the lookout for ways to make things work better.

♦ Be good at both establishing and following effective routines and
procedures. (This includes list-making, creating forms, record-
keeping, and similar skills.)

- ◆ Understand the importance of different kinds of maintenance, and schedule sufficient time for it.

- ◆ Know how to set limits and work within them.

- ◆ Be resourceful and resilient, making the best of things even when faced with seemingly insurmountable obstacles.

- ◆ Know when it's time to move on.

Chaos-Conquering Strategies

The chaos-conquering strategies that follow are variations of those I've developed over my 14 years as a professional organizer. I realize that consulting with Chaos Creators as I do for a few hours, or even a few days, is very different from dealing with your own chaos or working side-by-side with a Chaos Creator week in and week out. After all, I'm hired to give my opinion; you're often paid to keep yours to yourself. I serve as a catalyst, while you get to deal with the daily catastrophes.

So, keeping that in mind, I've modified my techniques into a sensible four-step process designed to help you conquer chaos, no matter who is causing it:

Step I: Document Disorder
Step II: Analyze Chaos
Step III: Plan a Strategy
Step IV: Facilitate Change

Step I: Document Disorder

The process of counteracting chaos begins with identifying and documenting the frequency, source, category, and costs of any chaos-causing acts.

The simplest way to do this is to detail the incidents of chaos by keeping a Chaos Log for at least two weeks. (You may want to copy the Chaos Log form or create your own version.)

Like anything worth doing, keeping a Chaos Log does require that

Chaos Log

Date/Time: _____

Name of Chaos Creator: _____

Type of Chaos Creator (e.g., DCC, CCC): _____

Description of Chaos: _____

_____

_____

_____

Chaos Category (Time, Memory, Communication, Information,

Project):_____

_____

_____

_____

Outcome/Time Wasted: _____

Estimated Value of Lost Time: _____

Victim(s): _____

you invest time to maintain it—but, as you'll see, it can really pay off. Especially when the chaos you're documenting is being created by people other than you. (Documenting your own chaos-creating ways is certainly useful, but it's not as much fun as keeping tabs on your chaotic coworkers.)

One of my favorite Chaos Log success stories was our Mess Maven friend, Lucy, mentioned in Chapter 2. I had met Lucy several years ago, after I got a call from a supervisor at the company where Lucy served as office manager. The supervisor, Karen, told me she thought Lucy was overwhelmed and needed to get more organized.

I spent some time at their company evaluating the situation, and I soon realized that the problem wasn't really Lucy. She was a classic Mess Maven—basically quite organized, but with a high-visibility messy desk. The real reason Lucy was overwhelmed, I discovered, was that she herself was the victim of Chaos Creators! Not only that, but one of her Chaos Creators was Karen—the same supervisor who had hired me to "straighten out" Lucy. (A challenging situation for me—but not an uncommon one, by the way.)

Lucy needed to prove that she was not the source of chaos in her department, despite her messy desk. (*Note:* A paper-flow system, like the one described previously in Chapter 7, ended up helping Lucy keep her desk looking tidier without sacrificing her effectiveness.) To help Lucy gather proof of who was really causing the chaos, I suggested she keep a Chaos Log for two weeks to document the recurring incidents and identify the perpetrators of chaos.

Step II: Analyze Chaos

After you've logged sufficient evidence of the chaos crimes, you can begin analyzing that data. Start by deciding which of the five chaos categories each incident of chaos belongs in (time, memory, communication, information, or project). Fill in the Chaos Category blank on each page in your Chaos Log. Then figure out how many chaotic incidents you have in each category.

Once you've done a breakdown (without, I hope, having one yourself), you'll see which category creates the most work. This, in turn, will enable you to focus on devising solutions.

Depending on your situation, you might also want to add up the estimated amounts of wasted time and costs of same. Use your judgment. Either way, that data might come in handy later.

On page 164 you will see two samples from Lucy's Chaos Log.

Once Lucy had collected her data, she analyzed it. Making a list of the Chaos Creators in her life, she noted the categories of chaos she experienced, and tallied the estimated costs to the company in hours and dollars. At this point, she told me she felt—for the first time—a sense of power, as though she could actually change her situation. (Lucy was becoming a Chaos Conqueror without even realizing it!)

Lucy's Chaos Log

Date/Time: *April 1   4:20–4:35 p.m.*

Name of Chaos Creator: *Karen*

Type of Chaos Creator: *DCC*

Description: *Karen asked Lucy to help locate a personnel file that Karen had misplaced.*

Chaos Category: *Information-related*

Outcome/Time Wasted: *Lucy located missing file (misfiled in wrong section) after 15 minutes.*

Victim(s): *Lucy*

Estimated Value of Lost Time: *$10*

Date/Time: *April 2   11:50 a.m.–12:15 p.m.*

Name of Chaos Creator: *Ralph*

Type of Chaos Creator: *CCC*

Description: *Ralph forgot to prepare (photocopy and staple) 30 handouts for a lunch meeting and asked Lucy to do it and then drop them off at the conference room because he (Ralph) was already late.*

Chaos Category: *Memory-related*

Outcome/Time Wasted: *Lucy spent 30 minutes (including half of her lunch break) photocopying, collating, stapling, and delivering the handouts.*

Victim(s): *Lucy, and the 30 meeting attendees who were kept waiting.*

Estimated Value of Lost Time: *$310*

Documenting disorder and analyzing chaos can be extremely useful to you in at least two ways:

1. If chaos-creating colleagues are the problem, and you'd like to see them receive a comeuppance (maybe they'll get transferred or even terminated), you may want to use your Chaos Log for as long as possible (not just two weeks) to create long-term proof of the problems. Putting the log to use in this way is not really vindictive—the purpose is just to keep an objective record of what's going on. But when the right opportunity presents itself, it's nice to have the evidence in hand to convict the culprits of chaos in the first degree. Whether you're in a position to fire the Chaos Creators yourself or you must report them to a higher authority, a well-kept Chaos Log will work in your favor.

2. If you're the Chaos Creator—or if someone else is, who you'd prefer not to eliminate—use the Chaos Log in a less subversive way. Employ it to pinpoint and prioritize specific, recurring chaos-causing actions and habits, so you can identify any patterns and thus strategize more effectively. The Chaos Log should show you exactly what you or your chaos-creating colleague is doing that makes your work difficult or demoralizing.

◆◆◆

When Incompetence Causes Chaos

Alas, some Chaos Creators are more incompetent than disorganized: they lack the necessary know-how to fulfill their job duties. If you're unfortunate enough to work with anyone like this, you have my sympathies. But at least your Chaos Log will get a good workout. (And who knows, you may even be able to publish it someday.)

◆◆◆

Step III: Plan a Strategy

Before deciding on your strategy, it's important to be clear, and realistic, about the results you want. Remember:

- ♦ If you're the problem, your objective should be to do your own job better so that you can keep moving onward and upward and also create less havoc for your coworkers.

- ♦ Coping effectively with other Chaos Creators involves changing how you relate to and deal with them, more than trying to change them. Even if you were able to make them organized, such a transformation would only be the means to an end.

The accompanying Focus Form is designed to help you clarify exactly what you want to gain from your efforts. Make a copy of it and fill it out now. To give you inspiration as well as insight, I've also included a copy of the Focus Form that Lucy completed.

The purpose of this form is to help you focus on why you wish to undertake a project, what you hope to achieve upon its completion, how you plan to accomplish it successfully, when you'd like to see it finished, to whom you can delegate aspects of it (or the entire project), and costs involved. Be as specific as possible.

It's not the easiest form you'll ever complete, but the time and thought you put into it will pay off in the long run. Why? Because filling out a Focus Form forces you to be crystal-clear about your expectations, which in turn helps you formulate your plan of action.

Now that you've figured out specifically what it is you hope to accomplish, you're ready to consider how to go about it.

Step IV: Facilitate Change

You can change yourself. You can also change how you relate to others. But trying to actually change anyone else is often futile. What you can do, however, is facilitate change. Facilitating change involves:

Focus Form

Purpose (Why): _____

_____

_____

Goal (What): _____

_____

_____

Plan (How): _____

_____

_____

Deadline/Timeline (When): _____

Delegation (Who): _____

_____

_____

_____

Costs Involved (Products or Services): _____

_____

_____

Benefit(s)/Reward(s): _____

_____

_____

_____

Lucy's Focus Form

Purpose (Why): *I want to make my life easier at work, reduce job stress and hours, and stop getting blamed for other people's chaos.*

Goal (What): *Get part-time clerical assistant.*

Plan (How):
(1) Use Chaos log to document problems for two weeks.
(2) Copy and distribute Chaos Log to staff at month-end meeting.
(3) Present options for improvement (review Miracle Worker's suggestions).

Deadline/Timeline (When): *By next month-end staff meeting (April).*

Delegation (Who): *N/A*

Costs Involved (Products or Services): *N/A*

Benefit(s)/Reward(s): *Eliminate unpaid overtime and resulting stress. I want to be able to eat lunch during my lunch break and leave work at 5:00 most days.*

1. Clarifying why specific types of change are desirable and necessary.
2. Making it as easy and appealing as possible to change the way things are done.

The following steps can help you ease into new habits and/or help you nudge others toward new ways of doing things without too much struggle and strife.

COMMUNICATE

If you haven't already communicated directly with your Chaos Creators about their chaos-causing habits, give the idea some serious thought. (If it's you who are the problem, this might simplify the task of communicating—especially if you like to talk to yourself.) Although I realize that articulating your concerns—whether via discussion or in writing—may not always be a comfortable or prudent option, it's still one worth considering. (At the very least, the image may cause you to burst into hysterical laughter.)

As an organizing consultant, the approach I use when communicating with Chaos Creators comprises a blend of straightforward suggestions and tactful advice, with a leavening dash of humor. But I, of course, get to leave at the end of a consultation or meeting; you, on the other hand, have to face the Chaos Creator (or look in the mirror) the next day, and the next, and the day after that. So you'll need to use your best judgment about when to be direct—and when to be diplomatic.

If you want to communicate effectively with Chaos Creators, the approach you choose will depend on three things:

1. Your job status in relation to theirs. (Are you higher, lower, or equal on the food chain?)
2. The nature of your professional relationship with them. (Friendly? Barely cordial? Frosty? Not on speaking terms?)
3. Which categories of Chaos Creators they represent: Deceptive (DCC)? Creative (CCC)? Oblivious (OCC)? Bureaucratic (BCC)?

Should you decide to speak with your Chaos Creators (as opposed to contacting them via written memo or e-mail), consider whether it would be more effective to meet with them one-on-one or in the presence of others (either in the context of a staff meeting, or a small group or team discussion). For an idea of how to conduct the latter option, read "The Saga of Lucy's Log, Continued," later in this chapter.

EDUCATE

"You can lead a Chaos Creator to order, but you can't make him think." But leading him (or her) there could be half the battle. (Again, if it's you who are the problem and you've read this far, presumably you're motivated.) Assume that your Chaos Creator has never been taught basic organizing skills, and prepare to provide helpful educational input.

In most cases, you won't actually be tutoring Chaos Creators overtly as much as feeding them useful information and ideas about getting organized. Although you can't force them to use those ideas, you'll at least be removing or reducing their excuse that they "just don't know how to get organized."

There are several ways to lead Chaos Creators to order, educationally speaking:

♦ Set a good example, and make a point of tactfully explaining how and why you organize.

♦ Give them an organizing book, audiotape, or videotape as a gift. Or if you're the problem, buy one for yourself to jump-start your own efforts at getting organized. (See Appendix A for suggestions.)

♦ Get them—and/or yourself—to take a class or attend a seminar. Even if you've concluded you're not the problem, you may want to go with them. You might get some more ideas yourself while giving the impression that you know you're not perfect either.

INNOVATE

Devise systems and procedures that work *with* chaos-creating habits instead of against them. Be sure to zero in on the area or areas in which you or the other Chaos Creator is most deficient: Is it management of time, memory, communication, information, or projects? (These are covered in detail in the preceding chapters.)

MOTIVATE

A key tactic for preparing to motivate yourself or others is to ask, "What's the payoff?" In order to become motivated, most people need to see a direct connection between improving their behavior and achieving benefits. Depending on your position and power in relation to theirs, you can offer various incentives for improvement:

♦ Awards

♦ Rewards

♦ Promotions

♦ Raises

♦ Bribes (not a recommended option in most cases)

Regularly provide positive reinforcement for any perceived effort to improve. Reward yourself with a fancy dinner out, a ticket to the ball game, a massage—whatever would be an unusual indulgence.

If it's someone else you're trying to help, enthusiastically express praise—especially within earshot of others. (But only if you sound wholeheartedly enthusiastic, not patronizing or pompous. An insincere inflection will cause this tactic to backfire.) Jot a note—even a Post-it scribbled with "Keep up the good work!" will make people aware that their efforts are noticed and appreciated, which can help to keep them motivated.

If you're in a position to influence an employee performance review, let a Chaos Creator know that his or her efforts to improve will have an impact.

The Saga of Lucy's Log, Continued

Armed with her Chaos Log data and her Focus Form-ulated goals and plan of action, Lucy was ready to do battle—er, facilitate change, that is. She had decided to communicate and educate by presenting her findings and suggestions for solutions at a staff meeting.

Since Lucy was not technically in a position of power, she opted for a diplomatic, non-confrontational approach. Before making copies of her Chaos Log to distribute to everyone at the staff meeting, she first covered up the names of the Chaos Creators. Then she practiced her presentation at home so she'd feel prepared (and less nervous). With the help of a paper-flow system I'd recommended, she also made an effort to keep her desk looking noticeably neater; this showed she had learned some pointers from our session, which bolstered her credibility as a newly proclaimed organized person.

At the meeting, Lucy distributed the Chaos Log copies, then stated her case. She didn't whine or place blame; instead, she pointed out that she was working to maximum capacity and essentially doing the work of two people—and she backed it up with specific examples. Lucy emphasized that the key reason she often came in early or stayed late to catch up was not her heavy workload; it was because of the way her time was being used by other staff members (documented in the Chaos Log). And she gently noted that her previously messy desk had been caused, more often than not, by other people dumping their chaos and clutter on her—although she made sure to take responsibility for some of it.

Lucy concluded by reminding them that my consultation overview report recommended either training these staff members to operate more effectively or hiring a part-time clerical assistant to enable her and the office to run more efficiently.

The result? Lucy was vindicated. Karen grudgingly agreed that a part-time helper was warranted, and a clerk was subsequently hired. And although Karen and the other Chaos Creators did not instantly become more organized, Lucy says they've made obvious efforts to improve.

Developing an Effective Approach

Keeping a Chaos Log may not solve all your Chaos Creator problems, but it will give you a valuable tool which can be used to help you construct a winning approach. Like any tool, however, it should be wielded with care, as Lucy did. You'll certainly need to adapt it to your needs. Lucy's tactics worked for her particular situation; but you may find, for example, that it wouldn't be appropriate—or effective—for you to publicly share your Chaos Log results.

Let's analyze how Lucy developed the approach she used to carry out her plan to facilitate change. First, she thought through her approach. She chose to communicate discreetly (instead of directly) at a staff meeting (instead of one-on-one with Karen).

Second, she set up her approach in advance. If she hadn't taken the time to cover up the names before distributing copies of the Chaos Log, her efforts could have backfired by creating resentment and embarrassment instead of acknowledgment and support.

Third, she practiced her approach. By rehearsing her presentation beforehand, Lucy knew she was prepared and therefore felt confident and organized—and behaved accordingly. (This was especially important when you remember that she was a Mess Maven and had not been perceived as organized by her supervisor and coworkers.)

Finally, Lucy focused her approach in a solution-oriented way. She didn't just dump the Chaos Log results on everyone without offering specific solutions to the highlighted problems. What's more, the solutions she offered were reasonable and provided a clear choice between

(1) other people agreeing to change their behavior or (2) hiring additional help. Of course, Lucy knew which option she preferred: filling out her Focus Form had helped her decide that the easiest, quickest, and most effective way to improve her job was to get a part-time helper. Her carefully planned approach, coupled with her newfound Chaos Conqueror attitude, helped her facilitate change and achieve that goal.

How to Avoid Sabotaging Your Approach

What if you've developed what should be a winning approach, but it's not working? Let's take a look at what can go wrong.

Perhaps you're technically doing everything right, but it's the *way* you're doing it that's wrong. Sometimes, it's not what you do but how you do it that spells the difference between success and failure. Here are five common mistakes to avoid.

1. **Acting superior.** (Related behaviors include acting like a mother, using sarcasm, teasing, officiousness.)

    Never approach a Chaos Creator with an obvious air of superiority. Nobody likes to be treated like an idiot. A patronizing air or condescending tone will get you resentment instead of cooperation. And just because you may not do this consciously doesn't mean you're not guilty of it.

    If you've developed a reputation for being well-organized, and take pride in it, it's possible that some people perceive you as having a holier-than-thou attitude. Be aware that you may inadvertently put organizationally challenged people on the defensive—especially Creative Chaos Creators (CCCs). Overcoming this misperception takes time, sensitivity, and self-deprecating humor.

    Tactic: When offering assistance to a CCC or most other types of Chaos Creators, use a neutral, nonself-congratulatory tone and choice of words. Avoid using "I." For example, instead of stating, "I've found the best way to do this is . . ." try asking something like, "If there was an easier/more effective way to do/accomplish that, would you want to know about it?" Notice that you're not suggesting that this way is best or even better; you're specifically saying "easier" or "more effective," words that imply a beneficial result. Be prepared to back up your claim with specific examples of benefits.

2. **Acting apologetic.** (Related behaviors include obsequiousness, sub-
   servience, groveling.)

   The flip side of acting superior is acting inferior. Beware the inclination to bend over backward so as not to appear like an "anal-reten-
   tive" know-it-all. By acting overly self-deprecating, you may end up
   giving an entirely different kind of negative impression. Women in
   particular have a well-documented tendency to apologize unnecessarily. It's common for many of us to murmur "I'm sorry" like a
   mantra, as though we're responsible for anything that goes wrong.
   This is a great way to undermine your credibility and establish a per-
   ception of weakness, especially if you're dealing with a Deceptive
   Chaos Creator (DCC). If you act as though you're unsure of your
   abilities and seem lacking in self-confidence, why should they feel
   obliged to listen to your suggestions?

   Tactic: DCCs have a knack for making other people look bad, so
   it's particularly important to do everything you can to appear cool,
   calm, collected, and competent when you meet with them. Practice
   behaving like a self-confident person; make an effort to reduce or
   eliminate self-sabotaging mannerisms such as laughing nervously,
   apologizing frequently, and/or avoiding eye contact. If possible, ask a
   friend to videotape you having a conversation to see if you display any
   of these confidence-masking habits.

   Banish any sense of self-doubt before meeting with a DCC or
   other type of Chaos Creator to discuss your anti-chaos strategies.
   Don't confuse self-assurance with arrogance; think "quietly powerful," not "tooting your own horn." Instead of mumbling, "I don't
   mean to appear critical or anything, but perhaps you might possibly
   consider changing how you do that and I'd be willing to help you, that
   is, if you don't mind. . . ," say something like, "Have you ever tried a
   different way of doing that? There's another (system/procedure) that's
   been proven to be more efficient. It could save you time and effort."
   Be ready to jump right in and show them how it works before they
   can think of a way to put you down or minimize your expertise.

3. **Acting tactless.** (Related behaviors include brutal honesty, rudeness,
   impolitic observations.)

   Sometimes Chaos Creators are so overwhelmed they seem to operate in a fog. You may feel a strong temptation to give them a good
   shake—if only figuratively. But tough-love tactics aren't appropriate

in the workplace, so resist the urge or you might end up doing more harm than good.

In short, temper justice with mercy. After all, some—but not all—Chaos Creators are acutely aware of their imperfections, and they may be struggling to get on track. So remember, a gentle boost is more effective than a kick in the pants. Sometimes a little empathy and kindness can go a long way.

Tactic: Instead of bluntly commenting, "Looks like you've been slipping lately!" within earshot of others in your workplace, you might offer to take them out for coffee, if appropriate; then, over dessert, bring the conversation around to the chaos problem. Depending on how tactful you choose to be, you may or may not want to bring up specific incidents of chaos. If it's a situation that calls for extreme diplomacy and you wish to appear empathetic, you could even say something like, "At my previous job I used to have a problem with (fill in the issue). Then I learned some tricks for dealing with it. I'd like to share them with you."

4. **Acting hypercritical.** (Related behaviors include blaming, nit-picking, nonconstructive criticizing.)

   If you've always been fairly well organized, you may have difficulty believing at times that a Chaos Creator's behavior isn't something he's doing just to make you crazy—particularly if you work with an Oblivious Chaos Creator (OCC). There will be moments when you are convinced that these chaotic impulses are part of a deliberate diabolical plot to destroy your mind, your career, and your ability to speak without clenching your teeth. (And if this were a movie instead of your life, you might even be right.)

   Get over it. Even when Chaos Creators are aware of just how organizationally impaired they are (and OCCs often haven't a clue), they are more to be pitied than hated. And if you can keep that in mind, you'll be more effective and less critical.

   Tactic: There's an old adage: "If you can't say anything nice, don't say anything at all." This can be difficult to remember when you're wading through piles in an OCC's office and come across the documents she was supposed to have forwarded to you two weeks ago, anchored by a piece of fossilized fruit. But it's still good advice.

   It also helps if you can cultivate a sense of humor (avoid heavy sarcasm) and force yourself to look on the bright side. (I never said it would be easy!) Instead of peevishly pointing out each and every chaotic transgression, focus instead on two things: the most important recurring problem at the moment, and any signs of improvement or efforts to improve—no matter how feeble they appear to you. Try to balance any negative comment with a positive observation.

Even though you may have a justifiable urge to snap, "No wonder you can't ever get me your paperwork on time; your desk is a total disaster! And your files are just as bad! And your blah blah blah. . . ," stop yourself. A more effective approach might be: "I'm glad we were able to locate this report. Now that we've solved that mystery, let's see if there's a way to improve on your current system." Don't recommend dynamite or a dump truck (unless you get along with the Chaos Creator really well and joke around a lot anyway).

5. **Acting idealistic.** (Related behaviors include wishful thinking, "savior syndrome," unrealistic planning.)

    Positive thinking doesn't mean you should be unrealistic. Chaos Creators will not magically become models of organization and order, no matter how hard you hope. If you have a rescuer complex (I call it savior syndrome) and are convinced that it is your God-given duty to save poor, disorganized wretches from their hellish existence, good luck. Your efforts are doomed. Chaos Creators are not caterpillars inside cocoons of clutter, awaiting the touch of your magic wand to turn them into neat little butterflies. Clear out your mental file drawers and get rid of any such misconceptions that may be lurking there.

    Replacing unrealistic expectations with realistic goals will help you cope more successfully with all Chaos Creators, but especially with Bureaucratic Chaos Creators (BCCs). BCCs are so used to operating chaotically, their chaos is almost like Linus's security blanket—smelly, yet oddly comforting. Remember that change is difficult for anyone; inertia is, after all, the strongest natural force. Therefore, your approach needs to be tailored to the results you can realistically expect. So choose your goals carefully.

    Tactic: To achieve success when working with BCCs or any kind of Chaos Creator, use the Focus Form to help you clarify your goals. It's the best way to eliminate any fuzzy thinking or misapplied efforts.

Reactions and Tactics for Dealing with Them

Your efforts to modify a Chaos Creator's behavior may be met with one or more of the following reactions:

Anger: "Who the hell are *you* to tell me how to operate?!"
Apathy: "Who cares—it's always been done this way."
Blame: "If it wasn't for that so-and-so, I could do it better."
Denial: "Me? I don't have a problem!"
Embarrassment: "I was hoping nobody would notice."
Excuses: "I can't help it because _____."
Resistance: "Just you try and make me change!"
Ridicule: "You're a fine one to talk!"

Use these tactics to deal with such reactions:

1. State the specific issue or problem.
2. Provide evidence.
3. Recommend options for solution.
4. Cite specific benefits.

Treat the problem as separate from the person. No one likes to be treated as though they don't know how to do something well, and Chaos Creators are no exception. So instead of focusing on their shortcomings, focus on the problem. If you're careful not to treat the person as a problem, it will be easier to focus on the issue.

I don't ask my clients "What's wrong?" or "Where's the problem?" Instead, I ask them to describe what they do and how they do it, and at various points during their descriptions of systems and procedures, I ask: "Is that working for you?" If the answer is yes, I have them continue. If they hesitate or say no, then I note where the problem is and come back to it later.

Cool-off Tactic

When working with Chaos Creators, it's possible that at some point you're going to be on the verge of losing your temper. The best thing you can do to remain in control is stay focused, no matter how irritating they get. How? Use the Focus Form to help you achieve a clear sense of purpose. Develop a laser-like ability to cut through the clutter that Chaos Creators generate both literally and figuratively. Practice guiding them—or yourself—back to the task at hand. Each time someone starts to go off on a tangent, gently refocus the activity toward the point. On occasions when they attempt to sidetrack you, calmly refuse to swerve. Whenever they start to lunge toward distractions and interruptions, quickly steer them back on course. If they try to induce an argument or start ranting, don't participate—just keep inexorably moving forward.

A personal note: For stress reduction, I've found that it's helpful to have a punching bag set up at home to help you unwind after a long day with a Chaos Creator. For added relief, get a picture of your tormentor to tape onto it.

Now you've learned the why's and how's of becoming a Chaos Conqueror, along with the four-step process for conquering chaos. You've also learned how to keep a Chaos Log and use Focus Forms to formulate a plan, as well as how to avoid sabotaging your approach. The next four chapters will show you additional tactics and techniques to help you carry out your plan—and become a Chaos Conqueror.

◆◆◆

Ten Rules for Coping with Chaos Creators

1. Be professional; set a good example.
2. Be respectful; don't patronize.
3. Be specific; don't generalize.
4. Make it easy.
5. Remind and reinforce.
6. Follow up.
7. Acknowledge discernible efforts.
8. Reward improvements.
9. Be patient.
10. Be persistent.

◆◆◆

9

When Deception Camouflages Chaos:

SOLUTIONS FOR DECEPTIVE CHAOS CREATORS

A half-truth is a whole lie.
—YIDDISH PROVERB

*P*erhaps you have a "favorite" kind of Chaos Creator, a particular trait type that you find especially irritating. For me it's the Deceptive Chaos Creator (DCC).

DCCs camouflage their chaos-causing habits by masquerading as people who have everything under control. They have different ways of creating this facade. For example, certain DCCs pretend to be very organized. (As you've probably guessed, these are the ones who annoy me the most.) I've encountered this type many times over the years in my line of work—and only a few of them were clients. The majority have been so-called "organizers" who somehow manage to cultivate a crisp and efficient image during meetings and media appearances, yet neglect to return phone calls or follow through on their commitments.

Such DCCs may be perfectionists who have difficulty prioritizing. They're apt to spend more time making things look "just right" than accomplishing any real work. DCCs like this tend to take great pains—and give them to others.

The reason DCCs who pretend to be organized are my personal pet peeve is because they give truly organized people a bad name. They accomplish this by helping to perpetuate the Stereotype of the Organized Person (SOP) discussed in Chapter 2: obsessively tidy and "anal reten-

DECEPTIVE CHAOS CREATOR

tive." Worse, they actually are organizing imposters who promote themselves as being organized even while they create chaos.

These DCCs are able to pass themselves off as organized by, for example, making a point of telling others about their favorite contact management software or showing off the latest trend in time management systems. ("I can't believe you've never heard of the DayDreamer System! It's the best one on the market. Yes, it's a bit pricey, but after all—I'm worth it.")

What's especially aggravating is when DCCs preen and promote

◆◆

DCC Traits Include . . .

◆ *Image-consciousness.* DCCs need to appear as though they have everything under control, but tend to value style over substance (e.g., keeping a super-tidy work space but not getting much work accomplished).

◆ *Deception.* To disguise their chaos-causing ways, DCCs use various coverup tactics (such as pretending to be highly organized or using charm and charisma).

◆ *Hypocrisy.* DCCs are quick to put down other people's efforts or point out mistakes, a tactic that draws attention away from their own.

◆◆

themselves as being organized—and get away with it because they look the part. Meanwhile, your desk gets swamped with all the stuff they dump on you. Their own desks may look neat on top, but don't be deceived. Beneath the well-polished surfaces, chaos churns. Debris-stuffed drawers, clutter-crammed credenzas, and filing systems from hell—even though you'd never know it to look at them or hear them talk.

I've also observed that DCCs routinely arrive unprepared for meetings and appointments—but they'll show up early, using their pre-punctuality like a prop to distract others from the truth. And when DCCs borrow materials (after saying something like "How could I have forgotten to bring the minutes? It's so unlike me") they rarely return them. Your initial attempt to get your stuff back may be met with

◆◆

DCC Time Trick

How do DCCs have the time to keep themselves and their surroundings so tidy-looking? By shoving off their messy projects onto others, of course!

◆◆

Can You Identify the Deceptive Chaos Creator?

NEAT NICK	ORGANIZED OLIVIA
Keeps messages and mail neatly stacked; may discard without responding	Returns calls and correspondence in a timely fashion
Shows up early but unprepared for meetings; uses extra time to straighten crooked pictures on walls	Takes time to prepare and follow up for meetings, appointments, and projects
To keep desk tidy, throws out everything but paycheck	Locates items and information quickly and easily

slightly scornful resistance—they'll coolly claim that they did return the borrowed item, somehow implying that you are the one who's at fault.

But the real danger of DCCs who mask disorganization with neatness is that they distract from their deception by putting down anyone who appears less tidy and "together" than they. Once you let them get away with this kind of behavior, you're in trouble. DCCs will then press their advantage: the putdowns will segue into blame-pinning before you realize what's happening. By then it's too late: the DCC's perfect persona has been established, and you've become the chaos scapegoat. (Mess Mavens who work with DCCs are particularly susceptible to this type of treatment.)

Some DCCs do have tools other than tidiness for covering up their chaos-causing ways. Charm, for example. (A certain high-ranking politician comes to mind.) Charming DCCs are particularly problematic not just because they have a tremendous capacity for generating chaos, but because of their skill at glossing over their escapades while smoothly transferring blame to others.

◆◆

"D" Is for Deceptive, Not Demonic

I don't mean to demonize DCCs (or, for that matter, any type of Chaos Creator). They usually don't intend to cause chaos and stress for others; their smokescreen tactics are probably motivated more by fear of failure than by deliberate, diabolical chaosplotting. But using deception—and hypocritical deception, at that—to bolster blame is a trait I find hard to excuse.

◆◆

The DCC Boss

Norman, for example, was the ultimate DCC boss. The owner of a small but successful clothing company, he looked like a poster child for perfectionism—every hair in place and catalog-crisp clothes. He kept his goatee and nails perfectly trimmed, and his frameless glasses were so clean you could barely tell when he had them on.

Norman's office resembled a magazine layout. His glass-topped desk sported a built-in, state-of-the-art computer screen, and nary a piece of paper or photo marred the glacial landscape. The credenza behind his desk was equally devoid of clutter: it held only a Lucite in-out box, and the trays were usually empty.

Norman's pride and joy was his customized planner, and he delighted in showing it off to anyone who acted the least bit interested. Like an evangelist, he spoke lovingly about his favorite software and other computer programs that he liked to credit with keeping him super-organized.

Ellen, Norman's new assistant, discovered the truth.

During her first weeks on the job, Ellen—who was quite organized herself—experienced several unsettling incidents. The worst was when she walked into his office at 4:30 on Friday for a scheduled end-of-the-week recap meeting and was met with an icy stare. "You're thirty minutes late," said Norman.

Momentarily nonplused, Ellen stammered that she thought she was on time and showed Norman her calendar with the meeting time marked as 4:30; she could have sworn that was the time he'd specified. "You must have heard me wrong," he stated smugly. "I know I told you four o'clock."

Ellen was devastated—her first week on the job as the assistant to a supposedly organized person, and she was screwing up. Maybe she wasn't as organized as she'd always thought. Gradually her self-doubts multiplied, and she found herself becoming increasingly defensive.

As time went on, however, Ellen started noticing cracks in Norman's facade of organization. At first she thought his lapses were exceptions, but eventually she realized they were the norm (or the "Norm").

For example, although Norman appeared to listen carefully during conversations and meetings, Ellen noticed he actually never paid much attention to what anyone else had to say. As a result, he only heard what he wanted to hear. The rest he ignored or, worse, misconstrued. Yet, because he had adopted the mannerisms and body language of a "good listener" (leaning forward in his chair, making constant eye contact, saying "mm-hmm" often), Norman was able to intimidate people into thinking they were the ones at fault.

Ellen also discovered that Norman was careless about noting his appointments and commitments in his super-duper time management system. He despised taking the time to make notes while he was talking; afterward he wouldn't always remember things accurately, but refused to admit it. Instead, he'd blame others for the ensuing mix-ups.

One day Ellen was telling the office manager about the latest Norman-caused chaos. "Oh, yeah, Norman does that kind of stuff a lot," the woman replied with a mirthless laugh. "But he's so organized he gets away with it!"

Ellen decided that to keep her job—and her sanity—she would need some advice on how to work with Norman, so she called me for some help.

Analysis:	DCC Boss
DCC:	Norman
Chaos Category:	Communication-related
Chaos Specifics:	Poor listening, communicating, and note-taking skills
Recommendations:	1) Mirroring 2) Clarifying
	3) Documenting

I recommended the following techniques to help Ellen succeed.

1. **Mirroring.** This is a communications technique whereby the listener echoes or repeats back instructions or requests issued by the speaker. *Example:* Norman says, "The meeting will be at four-thirty on Friday." Ellen responds, "4:30 on Friday." (Not, "Half-past four," or, "I'll be there.")

2. **Clarifying.** To eliminate assumptions (or misassumptions), you need to be alert to potential problems that can occur as a result of unclear communication. Clarifying through questioning is one good way to do this. *Example:* Norman says, "I need you to have the catalog copy finished by Tuesday." Ellen responds, "When you say 'finished,' which format do you mean—final or a draft you can respond to?" After Norman clarifies that part of his request, Ellen continues. "By what time next Tuesday do you need it?" Then she mirrors his response.

3. **Documenting.** PUT EVERYTHING IN WRITING. Yes, it takes time, but it will save endless hours of aggravation caused by misunderstandings. *Example:* After Ellen realized Norman was a lousy listener, she established a post-meeting ritual: she writes up a brief, bulleted summary of what was covered during the meeting and gives it to him within 24 hours.

   (*Note:* It's important not only to write things down in a systematic fashion but also to be obvious about it. Demonstrate your organizational habits by making a point of jotting notes in a log book or notebook anytime your DCC boss asks you to do something. This habit will establish you as a person to be reckoned with.)

Ellen found that, by consistently implementing these three procedures, she was able to work well with Norman. He, in turn, appreciated her organized ways, and eventually gave her this thought-provoking compliment: "Ellen, you're almost as organized as I am!"

The DCC Employee or Subordinate

Rachel, a publicist at a small public relations agency, was very good at writing error-free press releases. In fact, she prided herself on her ability to make everything she produced "look perfect." She was particular about every detail—and liked to let others know it.

Dana, who owned the agency, was initially impressed with Rachel's skills and her apparent professionalism. Extremely organized herself, Dana assumed that Rachel was, too. After all, Rachel was so neat, so concerned with getting things just right, so careful not to make mistakes—that's what being organized is all about, isn't it?

Well, *no.* As you now know, it's actually "more important to do the right thing than to do things right." But perfectionist DCCs often turn this truism inside-out, focusing on "doing things right" to the exclusion of doing the right thing.

In Rachel's case, this problem manifested itself as a time management issue. She spent so much time making sure each task was done perfectly that she was unable to complete all of her tasks. And sometimes the assignments she failed to finish were actually more important than those she completed so perfectly.

Dana realized that Rachel was neglecting a crucial area of her duties: media follow-up calls. Consistent follow-up is an essential step in effective publicity campaigns. Dana's agency had built its reputation on excellent follow-up. So here was a serious dilemma: Although Rachel was sending out first-class press releases and media kits, she wasn't following up by phone in a timely fashion.

Dana explained to Rachel that the value of her printed materials was essentially voided by her lack of telephone follow-up. She asked Rachel to make follow-up more of a priority than hunting for typos or perfecting an already adequate media kit. "Making a good impression is important," she told her, "but getting results is even more important. And follow-up helps to get results."

Rachel agreed to work on her follow-up procedures, and Dana felt optimistic. But as time went on, she could tell that little had changed. Rachel's follow-up efforts were still sketchy; when Dana asked her for updates, she was evasive.

Clients began to complain. Something was amiss—they were getting less media coverage than they had come to expect. And Dana found herself making excuses to them. Something had to be done. Should she fire Rachel? It was true her writing and promotional ideas were excellent. But if she couldn't or wouldn't do the follow-up that her job required, Dana worried, maybe she just wasn't the right person for this job.

Analysis: DCC Employee/Subordinate
DCC: Rachel
Chaos Category: Time- and communication-related
Chaos Specifics: Not allocating time for follow-up calls
Recommendations: 1) Scheduling   2) Scripting   3) Logging

Dana realized that Rachel was not a people person—she didn't really enjoy talking with people, preferring instead to work via computer and printed materials. In an ideal world, Dana could afford to keep Rachel plus hire another publicist to handle all the phone work. But reality dictated that if Rachel was to keep her job at Dana's small agency, she needed to overcome her follow-up phobia.

Dana chose to approach the problem as one relating primarily to time management; she felt that Rachel needed to schedule sufficient time to make follow-up calls. Since Rachel considered herself an organized person, Dana reasoned that she might respond well to a time management–related program for improvement.

1. Scheduling. Scheduling maintenance time for recurring tasks is crucial. As with structuring (page 194), scheduling involves planning a routine to ensure that sufficient time is set aside for specific activities. Scheduling is less detailed than structuring because it relates primarily to maintenance work, as opposed to projects and maintenance.

Example: Dana showed Rachel how she herself scheduled daily follow-up call time in her planner. "I even have a quota—twenty calls a day," she explained. "That's why I schedule a minimum of two hours each day just for follow-up." She made a point of being very specific with Rachel about how much time should be allocated for phone work. Dana also told her that if she could bring her follow-up skills on a par with her writing skills, she'd be eligible for a raise in two months.

2. Scripting. Telemarketing companies use scripts to train their employees on how to make sales calls. This method can be adapted for anyone who needs to make repetitive calls. Scripting doesn't necessarily involve reading a script word for word (which often creates a robotic impression). It actually works best when put in the form of an outline or even a checklist.

Example: Dana sat down with Rachel and went over, point by point, what needed to be covered in a typical follow-up call. Since Rachel's writing was her strong point, Dana asked her to write her own script, incorporating all of the key points. Rachel was then able to use her own words to help ease herself into the follow-up process. Rachel found that just having the script nearby when she made her calls helped her get the job done more efficiently. The script provided "focus points" and kept her on track. This gave her more of a feeling of being in control of the process, which in turn helped her to overcome her fear of it.

3. **Logging.** Keeping a log to track data is a time-tested way to measure input or output. Like documenting (see page 185), logging does take a bit of time and a certain amount of organization. But since DCCs pride themselves on being organized, keeping a log for a specific purpose is something they generally won't refuse to do. Some DCCs prefer using a notebook or binder, while others may use a favorite software program.

Example: At Dana's request, Rachel designed a Follow-up Call Log form and set up a binder for the log. Since she was a very detail-oriented person, keeping track of her calls was actually something she enjoyed doing.

Because Dana figured out how to use Rachel's strong points to counteract her weak points, she was able to help Rachel become a top-notch publicist. Rachel not only got the raise she'd been promised; she eventually went on to become a partner in Dana's agency.

The DCC Coworker

Dan, the managing editor of a regional magazine, thought he was very organized because he made a point of clearing off his desk at the end of each day, and he never went anywhere without his Day-Timer.

Actually, he was a good editor, extremely thorough and hardworking. But because Dan was such a perfectionist, he'd spend enormous amounts of time reshaping articles, double-checking the copy editor's work, and rewriting headlines.

Brian, the magazine's production manager, had the challenging task of getting the magazine to press on time each month, and he never missed a deadline. But he found himself becoming increasingly frustrated because Dan never got the copy in on time. So at the end of each month, Brian found himself with the Herculean task of having to organize a month's worth of work overnight, to make the printer's deadline.

Dan always had excuses. He blamed the writers, the events editor, and the copy editor for being slipshod and creating extra work for him.

But Brian felt that the problem was primarily caused by Dan's perfectionism, and ultimately his refusal to adapt to the reality of his job. A managing editor, Brian thought, didn't have time to obsess about every little comma and act like a prima donna. Instead, a managing editor was supposed to be able to process information effectively and efficiently, juggling multiple details without dropping any deadlines. Keeping a clear desk should be the least of his concerns—especially during the end-of-month crunch!

Analysis:	DCC Coworker
DCC:	Dan
Chaos Category:	Project-related
Chaos Specifics:	Difficulty balancing work flow
Recommendations:	1) Charting 2) Evaluating 3) Streamlining

Brian realized that Dan didn't want to own up to the fact that he was the one causing the problem. So Brian chose an approach he knew might appeal to Dan: he asked for his help.

1. **Charting.** A work-flow chart is a tool that can be used to help identify weak spots in the work-flow structure. It maps the specific steps and interactions by work role (not by individual), so participants can see how and where their specific efforts contribute to the overall process.

Example: Brian figured that a work-flow chart might give Dan an opportunity to see how and where he needed to change the process or pace of his editing output. He asked Dan to help him prepare one, ostensibly so that everyone in the editorial department could see where each person's work fit into the overall picture. (See Editorial Work-Flow Chart, page 190.)

2. **Evaluating.** Once the work-flow chart is completed, it's important to evaluate the steps of the work flow to pinpoint any potential problem areas.

Editorial Work-Flow Chart

WORK FLOW	DESCRIPTION
1. ME > WRI	ME assigns articles to WRI.
2. WRI > ME/EE > ME	WRI turn in assignments to ME; and EE turns in Events column to ME. (*Note:* Between assignment dates and deadline dates, ME edits existing articles and make assignments for future issues.)
3. TE < ME > EA	ME divides up articles among himself, TE, and EA. (ME and TE edit; EA inputs hard copy not submitted on disk.)
4. EA > ME	EA returns hard copy and disk to ME for editing.
5. ME > < TE	ME exchanges edited copy with TE (2nd-stage edit).
6. TE > ME	TE returns edited copy to ME.
7. ME > PUB/EE	ME distributes all edited copy to PUB and EE for final approval.
8. PUB/EE > ME	PUB and EE return corrected copy to ME.
9. ME > CE	ME sends corrected copy and disk to CE.
10. CE > ME	CE copyedits, then modems complete final copy to ME.
11. ME > PR	ME modems/downloads galley proofs to PR.
12. PR > ME	PR returns completed edition to ME.
13. ME > PM	ME modems/sends final proofs to PM.

Codes:
CE = Copy Editor
EA = Editorial Assistant
EE = Events Editor
ME = Managing Editor
PM = Production Manager
PR = Proofreader
PUB = Publisher
TE = Technical Editor
WRI = Writers

Revised Editorial Work-Flow Chart
(Revisions indicated by boldface)

WORK FLOW	DESCRIPTION
1. ME > WRI	ME assigns articles to WRI.
2. WRI > ME/EE > ME	WRI turn in assignments to ME; and EE turns in Events column to ME. (*Note:* Between assignment dates and deadline dates, ME edits existing articles and make assignments for future issues.)
3. TE < ME > EA	ME divides up articles among himself, TE, and EA. (ME and TE edit; EA inputs hard copy not submitted on disk.)
4. EA > ME	EA returns hard copy and disk to ME for editing.
5. ME > < TE	ME exchanges edited copy with TE (2nd-stage edit).
6. TE > ME	TE returns edited copy to ME.
7. ME > PUB/EE	ME distributes all edited copy to PUB and EE for final approval.
8. PUB/EE > ME	PUB and EE return corrected copy to ME.
9. ME > CE	ME sends corrected copy and disk to CE.
10. CE > **PM**	CE copyedits, then modems complete final copy to PM.
11. **PM** > PR	**PM** modems/downloads galley proofs to PR.
12. **PR > PM/ME**	**PR returns corrected galley proofs to PM and ME.**

Example: Brian met with Dan to evaluate the information outlined in the work-flow chart. They agreed that streamlining the steps could make both their jobs easier. Brian pointed out that the existing process created extra work for Dan because he was involved in literally every step. The extra work was taking up extra time, which in turn created the pressure-packed deadlines that were stressing both of them out.

Dan acknowledged the truth of Brian's observation. But he also expressed concern that the quality of their magazine would deteriorate if he were to "drop out" of any of the steps. Errors would slip by, he argued; this would reflect badly on the publication in general and his reputation as an editor in particular.

Brian told Dan that he understood his viewpoint, but he also noted a delicious irony: although Dan was a fine editor, he wasn't able to edit the work-flow process to eliminate backtracking and redundancies. He was too close to his work to see it objectively.

3. **Streamlining.** After identifying the redundant or inefficient steps in the work-flow process, it's possible to cut away the fat without damaging the muscle, so to speak.

Example: Brian offered to "edit" the editorial work-flow chart for Dan. He pointed out that, as production manager, he worked primarily outside the editorial process and therefore had a less subjective view of it than Dan. (See revised chart, page 191.)

The revised work-flow arrangement enabled Brian (the PM) to get his hands on the editorial copy earlier in the process (at Step 10 instead of what had formerly been Step 13) so that he didn't wind up having to do all the work at the last minute. Yet there was no question that Dan (the ME) still retained the lion's share of control over the editing process.

The DCC Secretary or Assistant

Jean was also a DCC, and she cost her boss, Erica, lots of time and frustration before she was discovered.

As property manager for a large condominium complex, Erica was quite organized, but the job grew so large that she became overwhelmed. Though she managed to keep the board of directors happy, her office had become cluttered from the backlog of paperwork waiting to be filed or shredded. Everyone agreed it was time for her to find an assistant.

Jean seemed perfect for the job. She loved "keeping things organized" and had a friendly yet business-like phone manner. Tidy, well-groomed, and perky, she looked to Erica like a workplace version of Mary Poppins.

Unfortunately, Mary Poppins never worked in an office. The first sign of trouble came when Jean took it upon herself to "organize" the office one weekend soon after she was hired. When Erica walked in the door on Monday, she almost fainted. The office looked as neat and tidy as Jean, but where had she stashed all the paperwork?!

Erica's carefully stacked piles, which she'd been slowly wading through, were nowhere in sight. Her desktop items had been completely rearranged, and the credenza surface was stripped bare of its well-thumbed reference volumes. Jean was beaming with accomplishment. "How do you like it?"

Restraining the urge to shriek, Erica replied that it looked nice, but what had become of her important papers and resource publications? Jean triumphantly opened the door to the storage closet, revealing several boxes of neatly stacked papers squeezed in between the vacuum cleaner and the coffee machine supplies.

Smiling weakly, Erica sat her assistant down and explained that in the future it would be better for Jean to check with her first before "organizing" anything. She didn't want to dampen Jean's enthusiasm or hurt her feelings, so she hid her rising panic (thinking, "My God! It'll take me *hours* just to find the paperwork I need to handle today!"). Nevertheless, Jean seemed somewhat miffed that her efforts weren't properly appreciated, and she assumed an injured air for the rest of the day.

Jean was good at maintaining the day-in, day-out office details: answering correspondence, filing, and returning phone calls. But over time, Erica noticed that projects she asked Jean to do weren't getting done on time. For example, one of Jean's duties was to input and mail out the minutes and agenda for the monthly board meeting. Yet board members started complaining to Erica that they weren't receiving anything until the meeting day.

When Erica brought up the issue with Jean, she was shocked to hear Jean deny that she was at fault in any way. Erica hadn't given her a realistic deadline for getting the mailing done, Jean claimed. Then she veered off in the opposite defensive direction, saying that she was actually only a day or so late getting the stuff in the mail; it was the post office that delayed things further.

All this left Erica wondering if perhaps Jean wasn't her ideal assistant after all. Maybe she should try to find someone else.

Analysis: DCC Secretary/Assistant
DCC: Jean
Chaos Category: Information- and project-related
Chaos Specifics: Poor prioritizing, judgment, and scheduling
Recommendations: 1) Structuring   2) Systematizing
                       3) Meeting

Erica decided that Jean's positive qualities outweighed her limitations. She realized that to make the most of Jean's potential she would have to work with her differently. The following methods enabled Erica to bring out the best in Jean and made both of their jobs easier.

1. **Structuring.** Certain people work well as long as they have a structure to cling to. Without boundaries of some sort to guide them, they're lost—but they don't know it.

Example: Erica had Jean map out a daily routine, with time allocated for various ongoing duties and projects. She also made up a calendar schedule for Jean to follow, with deadlines clearly marked for the entire year. Jean could see exactly what was expected of her, and when, so nothing was left to chance.

2. **Systematizing.** Following established systems and procedures is different from creating them. DCCs often think that because they're good at coloring within the lines, they're good at drawing. But usually this is not the case. Therefore, you need to set up specific systems and devise clear procedures for them to operate.

Example: Erica set up a tickler file system for Jean to use, with daily and monthly files. She made 8 × 10-inch "reminder cards" for each recurring monthly project (such as "Board Meeting Preparation"), explaining to Jean that the cards should be moved ahead, month by month, as each project was completed.

3. **Meeting.** Regular "touch points" are helpful to ensure that things aren't slipping through the cracks. A beginning-of-the-day briefing and/or a weekly debriefing make it unlikely that a DCC can claim not to have understood what was expected of him or her.

Example: Each morning, Erica briefly outlines to Jean her priorities for that day. Erica's briefing includes not only Jean's to-do's but her own as well, so that Jean is always informed of Erica's schedule. The briefing also gives Jean the opportunity to bring up any questions or "leftovers" from the previous day.

Working with Jean has forced Erica to become more organized herself. It has also made her understand that there are a variety of ways to be organized. Erica and Jean are now able to work together as a team to keep the office running smoothly.

General Advice for Coping with DCCs

1. Never appear awed or intimidated by a DCC's perfectionism.
2. Don't do their work for them.
3. Find ways to make the most of their orderly tendencies.

10

When Creativity Condones Chaos:

IDEAS FOR CREATIVE CHAOS CREATORS

I'm chaos and he's mayhem. We're a double act.
—RIGGS (MEL GIBSON) IN LETHAL WEAPON 3

Style-wise, at least, Creative Chaos Creators (CCCs) are the complete opposite of Deceptive Chaos Creators: Instead of hiding their disorganization, they appear to flaunt it. In fact, they're apt to festoon their cluttered work areas with paperweights, pins, and other paraphernalia proclaiming credos like "A Neat Desk Is the Sign of a Sick Mind."

CCCs tend to describe themselves as "artistic" or "creative" in an effort to excuse their chaotic ways—but for some, excuses are the most

CCC Traits Include . . .

- *Messiness.* CCCs seem to revel in disarray and are comfortable with clutter.

- *Excuse-making.* To justify their chaos-causing ways, CCCs claim that their creativity is at fault—they "just can't help it."

- *Humor.* CCCs often poke fun at themselves and tend to laugh off criticism.

CREATIVE CHAOS CREATOR

creative things they produce. Their alibis, however, often go unchallenged because of the widespread acceptance of "creative" as a politically correct euphemism for both "messy" and "chaotic." This creative chaos phenomenon accounts for why silly sayings such as "a creative mess is better than tidy idleness" are accepted as humorous truths.

There is, however, something innately humorous about the creativity = chaos school of thought. In fact, if this school had a student

Creating Chaos Does Not Make You Creative

I'm not denying that the creative process can be chaotic at times. My point is that being creative is not a valid excuse for continually causing chaos for yourself and others. There are many highly accomplished creative people who are either organized and neat, organized and messy (e.g., Mess Mavens), or simply successfully disorganized—able to function well despite their disorganization.

body, CCCs would be voted Class Clown—they can make it seem as if being "organizationally impaired" is hilarious. These fun-loving and often funny people may get us to laugh even as they make our lives difficult. I think they're the most likeable kind of Chaos Creator, if for no other reason than that they're not afraid to poke fun at themselves and their disarray.

But no matter how endearing they can be, CCCs can't stretch their appeal enough to cover the chaos they continually create and the problems it causes. These perpetually scattered folks frequently comment that they're always "putting out fires," and may absently wonder aloud why they consistently run "a day late and a dollar short." Their basic problem is an unwillingness to admit that having a creative nature is no excuse for chaotic and irresponsible behavior. But CCCs prefer to believe that getting organized would stifle their creativity.

The CCC Employee

Some CCCs are actually embarrassed by their disorderliness and would like to get organized, yet (like most people) are afraid to admit they need help. But Kevin, a 21-year-old whiz-kid software designer, wasn't one of them.

Terri, the hard-driving founder of a successful multimedia software development company, found this out when she stole Kevin away from his previous employer by offering almost double his previous salary.

Terri was practical and highly focused—in her own words, "super-organized"—and was often disdainful of anyone whom she perceived as disorderly. Then she hired Kevin. Though just past his teens, he was already widely regarded as something of a genius in the industry. But he had worked for only one other company before, Terri's chief competitor.

Kevin reveled in his reputation as an eccentric. He considered himself the Mozart of multimedia software, and acted like it was his duty to flaunt his idiosyncrasies. These included a penchant for wearing novelty hats (he was particularly fond of a baseball cap sporting a rather dusty pair of fake antlers) and a startling habit of crowing like a rooster whenever he completed a project or solved a problem to his satisfaction.

Kevin also insisted on going barefoot inside his "lair," as he referred to his office. He lost no time in cluttering the room with computer gizmos, an old guitar, an explosion of papers, a skateboard, and a curious assortment of windup toys. Within a week of his moving in, Kevin's lair resembled a computer nerd's version of Animal House.

Of course, when Terri hired Kevin she knew he was as famous for his quirks as for his work. But she wrote them off as immaturity and resolved not to let his wild style bother her, as long as he delivered the goods. However, she hadn't taken into account the fact that Kevin was almost an idiot savant when it came to functioning in the business world: aside from his multimedia design brilliance, he had virtually no understanding of even the most mundane office systems and procedures. Since he'd held only one other job, he was essentially a workplace Wild Child.

Terri soon discovered that Kevin had never used a filing system, let alone set one up for himself. His file drawers were empty save for some old fast-food wrappers and a comic book or two. He used the floor as a horizontal filing gallery, covering almost every square inch with individual sheets of paper so he could "see them." Yet he always maintained a clearly defined pathway from the door to his main computer station and desk.

Kevin's bookshelves looked like a lunatic's library. Manuals, binders, magazines, and disks were leaned against or stacked atop each other in no apparent order, although Kevin claimed he could always find what he needed . . . sooner or later. Occasionally one of the more precariously arranged piles would spontaneously self-destruct with a small crash, to his apparent delight.

For Terri, the overall effect was nightmarish. What most concerned her wasn't so much the appearance of Kevin's lair (although it did bother her) but the fact that it sometimes took him too long to find something someone else requested. "Chill out," he'd say as he rooted around on the floor, looking for a requested document. "It's around here somewhere—I just saw it the other day."

Anticipating future problems, Terri called me to come in and rescue Kevin from himself. "He needs help but he doesn't know it," she warned me.

Analysis:	CCC Employee
CCC:	Kevin
Chaos Category:	Information-related
Chaos Specifics:	Ignorance of workplace systems and procedures; lack of systems for papers and publications
Recommendations:	1) Educating 2) Innovating 3) Assisting

1. **Educating.** Ignorance isn't always bliss. When employees have no idea what they're expected to know, it can be frustrating both for them and for the people they work with. That's why it's important to take the time to explain the whys and whats of systems and procedures that may seem obvious to you but not to them. And it's equally important to ask them questions so you can educate yourself about their perspective as well.

Example: To start with, I asked Kevin to describe how he was currently organizing his paperwork so I could better understand his way of thinking. I figured he probably had some type of system worked out that was obvious only to him, and I was right.

He showed me that any papers he was working on at the moment were always kept right on his desk; papers he wasn't working on at the moment but that he anticipated needing in the near future were spread out on the floor under the desk, within kicking distance of his bare feet. And periodically he'd actually put certain papers ("ones I don't need to see anymore") in unlabeled manila file folders. Then he'd stick these back on the floor in one special corner of the room.

The only problem with this system, Kevin admitted cheerfully, was that there just wasn't enough floor space to spread out every single piece of paper. So, he had to overlap them. It was the overlapping, he confided, that caused him to misplace things.

I gave Kevin a crash course in organizing filing systems and paper flow, showing him sample systems and demonstrating how they might work for him. He listened politely (although he kept fidgeting with a windup shark), then made a revealing comment.

"I've always wondered how you find things in files," he said. "I mean, you put papers behind each other. How are you supposed to see them?" Good question. I explained to him that the labeled tabs are designed to indicate the contents of each file. However, I acknowledged that for some people, labels just don't provide sufficient clues. And I knew from talking to him that Kevin was probably one of those people.

2. **Innovating.** Trying to force someone to use a system that seems alien to the way they think is often unproductive. It's more effective to work with their natural tendencies instead of fighting against them. Resourceful thinking leads to innovative solutions.

Example: I suggested to Kevin that he might consider using the walls instead of the floor as a base for his paper system. He could even categorize his papers on giant corkboards, each with a different color frame or a large label to identify the category. Kevin liked this concept and decided to give it a try, much to his boss Terri's amazement.

Another recommendation he agreed to test utilized clear plastic stacking trays to keep "hot projects" close at hand instead of close to his feet. This option enabled him to use vertical space on his desk without actually piling papers.

For his periodicals and other bookshelf-stored items, I suggested he get some clear plastic "magazine butlers." These vertical holders keep softbound materials standing upright and allow easy access and visibility—points that were important to Kevin.

3. **Assisting.** Not everyone is capable of keeping things organized without some form of ongoing assistance; many CCCs, in fact, need help. So depending on your particular situation, you may want to look into the possibility of arranging for someone to come in and help maintain order on a regular or occasional basis.

Example: Kevin was never going to be a model of organization—after all, his talents lay in other areas—but he was willing to accept help. Therefore, I recommended that Terri arrange to have her administrative assistant stop by Kevin's lair once a week to assist him with his backlog. This way there would be someone in the company aside from Kevin who would be familiar with his systems and could locate things in his office for others if necessary.

Finding ways to work with Kevin's quirks was challenging but ultimately worthwhile. Acknowledging his way of seeing things as valid was an important part of opening the door to his "organized self."

The CCC Assistant

Nikki was the assistant to the top headhunter at a busy executive recruiting firm. Nikki functioned as Carla's "ear to the ground," and liked to share the latest office scuttlebutt and the best (or worst) jokes. She was also an aspiring artist who loved to decorate her desk with her work and loved it whenever anyone complimented her on it.

Providing entertainment was something Nikki liked to do. And she was one of the few people who knew how to make Carla laugh. In fact, she was often the butt of her own jokes, laughing about her disorganization and how she often messed up Carla's messages.

To Carla, however, it was not always a laughing matter. Nikki's habit of abbreviating messages and sometimes inadvertently editing out important details really bothered her and had put her in some embarrassing situations. Many times she had returned phone calls only to discover she wasn't prepared to give the caller the information she or he had requested via Nikki.

Nikki also seemed to have trouble asking Carla to go back over some information or explain something she didn't "get" the first time around. Since Nikki was afraid Carla would think she was dumb, she'd pretend to understand everything and then later try to work it out herself—often unsuccessfully.

Carla's frustration kept mounting. She didn't want to fire Nikki; she genuinely liked her and was happy with much of her work. Yet, as Nikki herself feared, Carla was getting fed up with her ongoing lapses. Finally, Carla called me to come in and help her and Nikki solve these challenges.

Analysis:	CCC Assistant
CCC:	Nikki
Chaos Category:	Communication-related
Chaos Specifics:	Mis-edits incoming messages; misunderstands directives; won't ask for clarification
Recommendations:	1) Automating 2) Clarifying 3) Encouraging

1. **Automating.** Some people just aren't good at taking messages, and aren't really interested in improving. Therefore, expecting them to develop their skills in this area may be unrealistic. A more effective approach might be to implement an automated system for message taking, freeing them to use their time and energy for those tasks they excel at.

Example: I suggested that Carla get a voice mail system to relieve her from depending on Nikki's message-taking ability. Initially she was reluctant to try this option, saying she "hated" voice mail. So I asked her which she thought was more frustrating: getting inaccurate messages from a human or complete messages from an automated system. She hesitantly agreed to give it a trial run. She and Nikki were both pleased with the results.

2. **Clarifying.** Communication assumes comprehension. Yet when one person speaks quickly and another hears slowly, gaps occur and miscommunication follows. Listeners who have trouble comprehending directives the first time around should be encouraged to speak up and request clarification of whatever didn't register clearly.

Example: Carla agreed to make a conscious effort to slow down when giving Nikki instructions. Nikki swore she'd speak up whenever she felt unclear about anything Carla asked her to do. However, she was concerned that doing so might cause Carla to treat her "like a dummy." Carla promised to be more patient, provided that Nikki demonstrate improved listening skills. I suggested Nikki try rephrasing Carla's directives, instead of just repeating them back, to show that she was actually paying attention. This solution proved to be effective.

3. **Encouraging.** Criticizing rarely achieves positive results, especially when the person being criticized has low self-esteem to begin with. Encouragement and positive reinforcement are preferable alternatives.

Example: Without coddling or patronizing her, Carla worked on bolstering Nikki's self-image by encouraging her to explore new outlets for her artistic abilities. She arranged for Nikki to take a graphic design workshop, and then suggested that she revamp various company materials. (Carla was cautious, however; she didn't want Nikki to get so involved in creative endeavors that she wouldn't be able to handle her other duties.) The result? Nikki blossomed. Her overall performance improved because she felt more confident of her own worth.

Carla's willingness to develop Nikki's potential paid off for both of them. Together they were able to evolve a working relationship that reduced chaos and encouraged creativity.

The CCC Client

Ed, the owner of a small bookkeeping firm, was well-organized and a stickler for detail. He knew how to keep his clients happy, and they all responded in kind. Except Ross—"the Client from Hell" (as Ed thought of him).

A middle-aged bachelor, Ross lived off a trust fund inherited from his parents. Since he didn't have to work, he spent most of his time wasting other people's time—or so it seemed to Ed. Wildly disorganized (and apparently proud of it), comically funny, generous to a fault, and perpetually self-indulgent, he seemed to reel from one chaotic episode to another like a character in a soap opera.

Ross was also a soft touch for any charity that rang his bell asking him for money. Unfortunately, he wasn't very discriminating about which organizations he donated to. He confided to Ed that he actually had "charity goons" harassing him—calling him at all hours and knocking at his door to pick up checks. When Ed checked out some of these "charities," he was horrified to discover most of them were frauds.

Unlike many of Ed's clients, Ross had both the money and the time to pay bills; he just didn't like to do it. When he first came to Ed, three different collection agencies were after him due to his unfortunate habit of sticking most bills under his bed and forgetting about them. He even boasted of having had his electricity shut off as a result of neglecting to pay the utility charges for several months.

Ross claimed he was ready to turn over a new leaf, and asked Ed to help him get his bills paid on time, keep his finances on track—and have his name taken off all the "sucker lists" of questionable charities.

Initially Ed was delighted to be of service. Charity goons aside, Ross's life appeared relatively simple, especially when compared to most of Ed's other clients: no business to manage, no payroll to handle, no tenants to collect rent from, no estate to settle, no foundation to administer, no family to care for . . . just bills to pay and plenty of money to pay them with.

But Ross had a way of making simple things complicated. He was so scattered, even the most basic projects disintegrated into chaos in his hands. It was always the same: Twice a month, Ed would call Ross a few days before his scheduled appointment, reminding him to get his paperwork together. (Ross insisted on coming in every two weeks, even though Ed thought once a month should be sufficient.) Ross would promise to follow through.

On the day of the appointment, Ross never failed to come dashing through the door 10 minutes late. Clutched in his arms would be a food-stained carton overflowing with bills, receipts, and financial statements mixed together with takeout menus, pizza coupons, travel brochures, postcards, candy wrappers, and, on one occasion, a dirty sock.

Then he'd sit down with Ed and start making jokes—and excuses.

"Just got over the flu," or, "I've been out of town a lot." Or even, "I had it all in order and then my housekeeper mixed everything up." Sooner or later, though, Ross would sheepishly confess that "I just need to get more organized." Yet he wasn't willing to have anyone come in and help him, and he couldn't seem to make any progress on his own.

But what bothered Ed the most was that Ross always hung around the office, pacing, goofing off, and chattering ceaselessly while Ed put the mess in order and got the work done for him. Ross's presence was distracting to Ed, and he'd end up spending more time than he wanted to on Ross's paperwork.

Ed's polite attempts to get Ross to quiet down or go away were always ignored, and he was afraid to be more assertive for fear of hurting the man's feelings. So he'd end up gritting his teeth (a headache-maker) and backing off.

Ed finally realized Ross was never going to be able to regularly pull together his paperwork and would always be something of a pest. Ross couldn't seem to help his "problem child" persona, but he was also basically a nice person. Annoying and frustrating, yes, but essentially good-natured, funny, and kind. Ed liked him and wanted to help him. He decided that, properly handled, Ross could be an excellent client. So changes would have to be made in how he worked with him.

Analysis:	CCC Client
CCC:	Ross
Chaos Category:	Project-related
Chaos Specifics:	Inability to organize materials; dependent personality
Recommendations:	1) Streamlining 2) Establishing boundaries 3) Gap-filling

1. **Streamlining.** By eliminating unnecessary steps in a necessary process, projects become easier to accomplish.

Example: To get the bills situation under control, Ed gave Ross two options. He could either arrange to have most of the bills paid electronically or have the bills sent directly to Ed for payment. Either way would eliminate the need for Ross to actually touch the bills.

At first, Ross was reluctant to choose either option. He disliked the idea of having funds removed electronically from any of his accounts. "What if they take out too much? I'd get taken to the cleaners," he argued. And the idea of having any of his mail rerouted to another address made him feel only slightly less uncomfortable. But Ed patiently discussed all the pros and cons of both ideas with him, and gently explained that doing things the old way was simply not an option anymore.

Eventually, Ross agreed to have the bills forwarded to Ed's post office box. And within a couple of months, things were running so smoothly he couldn't remember why he'd had a problem with the idea at all. Needless to say, Ed was pleased, and relieved.

2. **Establishing boundaries.** Because CCCs tend to be friendly and gregarious, they have a way of wrapping themselves around your time and space and squeezing out your energy. So it's important to set boundaries with such people in order to protect yourself. Remember, no one can take advantage of you without your permission. Setting limits helps you maintain control.

Example: Ross was basically a lonely person with too much time on his hands. His appointments with Ed were, for him, a social event. Ed—kind-hearted soul that he was—felt sorry for Ross, but he finally got to the point where he just didn't have the patience to deal with his shenanigans. After Ross's bills began coming directly to Ed, it seemed obvious that twice-a-month appointments were now completely unnecessary. Yet Ross still wished to stick with the old schedule, ostensibly because he had various financial statements (banking and brokerage) that he wanted Ed to go over with him.

Ed established his boundaries by explaining the following rules to Ross in a friendly yet business-like manner:

◆ He would meet with Ross regularly, once a month, for two hours, which should be sufficient for them to cover everything they needed to go over. (Ed also had figured out that two hours was the maximum amount of time he could stand to spend with Ross without developing a headache.)

◆ Additional appointments could be scheduled subsequently if Ross desired. (Ed reckoned he could always tell Ross he was all booked up but would call him if there was a cancellation.)

3. **Gap-filling.** Sometimes setting boundaries involves pulling back, which can create gaps. If you have been fulfilling a client's needs—tan-

gibly and intangibly—and then you pull back (to conserve yourself), it's a good idea to offer the person other options to fill those gaps. Not only will this help maintain the relationship, it can also strengthen it.

Example: Ed could see that what Ross really needed was a part-time assistant to help him keep his household running smoothly and also provide some companionship. Ed happened to know a retired secretary who had mentioned she'd like to do some part-time work.

Since Ross had, in the past, seemed resistant to the idea of having someone help him get organized, Ed didn't bring it up again. Instead, he arranged to have the woman drop by the office when Ross was there because he had a hunch Ross would get along well with her. Ed's hunch was correct, and once the ice was broken he had no trouble pitching the idea to Ross. The arrangement worked out beautifully for all three of them.

Stepping back to view the big picture allowed Ed to find solutions not only for himself but for Ross as well. By looking at Ross's needs with both clarity and compassion, he was able to change the dynamics of their relationship from irksome to ideal.

The CCC Partner

Steve and Joe, brothers and partners in a wholesale sporting goods business, were a good team overall. They had complementary traits and skills: older brother Steve, in charge of purchasing, was orderly, methodical, and mild-mannered; "Little Joe" (as he was known to family and friends) was outgoing, energetic, and somewhat scattered. He served as the sales director.

But Joe had one habit that got on Steve's nerves continually: he refused to write things down. When he did, he'd often forget what he'd done with the piece of paper. Steve blamed it on Joe's "hurry-scurry" attitude. Joe always acted like he was in a rush, even when he had no reason to be. That was just his style—revved up and high energy. He thought fast, talked fast, walked fast, drove fast—and forgot things fast.

True, it hadn't always been that way. Steve used to envy Joe's ability to remember names, faces, numbers, directions . . . everything. He just needed to hear or see something once, and that was it. Joe's memory was prodigious, something he was justifiably proud of. Yet he took it for granted, too. And like many people with excellent memories, he was just a tiny bit scornful of those lesser mortals who had to write things down. "What a waste of time!" he would mutter to himself impatiently while waiting for Steve to finish jotting something in his planner.

Joe's cluttered office reflected his whirlwind style. Product samples were strewn everywhere, intermingled with an eclectic assortment of gag gift items and stress-relieving devices—including a dartboard posted above the door.

After Joe hit his thirties, his memory started to slow down—but Joe didn't. He still kept up the same frenetic pace, perpetually rushing onward to the next idea, task, person, meeting, or event. Only now his mind, which had become as cluttered as his office, was starting to let things slip through the cracks, much to his dismay—and initial denial. Joe found himself forgetting appointments, prices, and other important information that he'd never had trouble remembering before. "I'm getting early Alzheimer's," he'd say half-jokingly as he apologized for his latest memory lapse.

The trouble was, since Joe had never gotten in the habit of writing things down, he didn't seem able, or willing, to start now. And, after all, he'd always made fun of people like Steve who wouldn't be caught dead without their Day-Timers. He still felt as though it took too much time to write things down, and he chafed at the thought that perhaps he was doomed to become like the "Planner Peanuts" he'd derided in the past.

But Joe finally got to the point where he was almost as fed up as Steve. He realized it was time to stop deluding himself that his memory was going to return to its previous sharp state—those days were gone. Yet the thought of constantly having to make notes made him feel discouraged and overwhelmed. Steve saw that Joe was ready to make some changes, and offered to help him.

Analysis:	CCC Partner
CCC:	Joe
Chaos Category:	Memory-related
Chaos Specifics:	Forgets appointments and other information; hates to write things down
Recommendations:	1) Accepting 2) Researching 3) Experimenting

1. **Accepting.** One person's life raft is another's lead balloon. That's why it's crucial you not assume that whatever works well for you should work just as well for someone else—especially if that someone else has a workstyle different from yours. Remember, a willingness to accept help does not necessarily translate into a willingness, or ability, to change.

Example: Steve made the mistake of first getting Joe a notebook planner just like his own. Joe tried to use it but gave up quickly, finding it cumbersome and frustrating. "It's no use," he told Steve. "I'm never going to be comfortable with something like this; it makes me feel like I'm back in junior high." Steve listened to Joe's comments without arguing or trying to change his mind. He thought about his brother's workstyle and concluded that Joe probably needed something that didn't actually involve writing things down.

2. **Researching.** Modern technology continues to evolve, offering us an ever-changing infinity of problem-solving options. It can be worthwhile to research the latest memory management tools not only for the purpose of helping someone else, but also because you might discover something of use for your own needs.

Example. Since Joe and Steve agreed that a notebook or binder-style product was out of the question, Steve decided to research some high-tech options instead. The newest electronic organizers and Personal Digital Assistants looked promising; he even found one he liked for himself. But there was nothing that seemed right for someone like Joe, who hadn't ever really gotten comfortable with computers. "Keying in a note takes me even longer than when I write it down," Joe complained. "I'll never use this." Then he said something that gave Steve an idea. "What I want is something I can talk into," Joe commented. "So I can do it while I'm walking or driving." Steve realized that all Joe really needed was some type of small recorder. He found several voice-memo devices that seemed ideal.

3. **Experimenting.** Once you've done the research and narrowed down the field of possibilities, it's time to actually test your choices. Since many products these days come with a money-back guarantee, what have you got to lose?

Example: Joe initially chose a credit card–sized recorder with only two buttons because it was the simplest to use. But after trying it for a couple of weeks, he found that it was too simple for his needs. Discouraged, he took it back.

Steve suggested he try a slightly larger one with a few more options. "What you need is something that lets you retrieve information fast, not just record it fast. It has to function like a reminder as well as a recorder." They settled on the Executive Voice Organizer because it had a small LCD screen for displaying information such as phone numbers and appointment dates and times—the types of things that Joe had been forgetting. He could access anything just by speaking into the machine, and also record messages to himself. Joe could hardly wait to start using it. And it turned out to be just what he needed.

Working together to find a solution to Joe's memory management problem helped strengthen Steve and Joe's partnership. And Steve became even more organized himself by helping Joe get organized.

General Advice for Coping with CCCs

1. A good sense of humor will come in handy.
2. Use positive reinforcement often.
3. Creative or innovative solutions are prized by CCCs.

11

When Oblivion Compounds Chaos:

HELP FOR OBLIVIOUS CHAOS CREATORS

When a man points a finger at someone else,
he should remember that four of his fingers
are pointing at himself.

—LOUIS NIZER

*O*blivious Chaos Creators (OCCs) don't have a problem—chaos *just happens* to follow them!

If their desks are disasters, it's their secretaries' faults. When a meeting they're in charge of runs an hour over schedule, it's because someone else talked too much. If they fail to respond to phone calls or faxes, it's because they didn't receive the message or "nothing came through." Some of my most challenging clients are OCCs, because they never contact me themselves. Instead, I get called in by their bosses and colleagues to help counteract the chaos caused by these oblivious beings.

Denial works in different ways. While some OCCs consciously ignore the havoc created by their disorganization, others are truly oblivious. They're myopic about the mess that surrounds them and may be genuinely puzzled by the chaotic circumstances they've created. But that doesn't make it any easier for you to work with them.

OCCs are expert excuse makers. This reason alone may explain why many OCC types often manage to achieve positions of authority and eventually become truly monstrous purveyors of chaos. (Not that I'm going to name any names here, but all you have to do is read any newspaper article datelined Hollywood or Washington, D.C.)

OBLIVIOUS CHAOS CREATOR

OCC Traits Include . . .

♦ *Hyper-focusing.* OCCs often get very absorbed in whatever they're working on, and this tunnel vision tendency—while useful in some ways—blinds them to their own chaos-causing habits.

♦ *Denial.* Because they don't or won't see how they are contributing to chaos, OCCs deny responsibility and blame others.

♦ *Pride.* OCCs tend to have big egos and do not handle criticism well (they can dish it out but they can't take it).

When Oblivion Is a Symptom

For some OCCs, it's not just a matter of making excuses; they seem to truly forget that they've made appointments or scheduled deadlines. In some cases, in fact, their behavior can even mimic the symptoms of the onset of Alzheimer's disease. Check the following warning signs (from the National Alzheimer's Association).

♦ Recent memory loss that affects job performance

♦ Misplacing things in inappropriate places

♦ Difficulty performing familiar tasks

♦ Disorientation of time and place

♦ Problems with abstract thinking

♦ Changes in mood or behavior

♦ Poor or decreased judgment

♦ Problems with language

♦ Changes in personality

♦ Loss of initiative

If you're concerned that you or your Chaos Creator may be exhibiting too many of these symptoms, you may wish to contact your local Alzheimer's Association office for advice. For your ordinary OCCs, however, there are other strategies worth exploring.

The OCC Client

Diane, the owner of a desktop-publishing business, almost had to relinquish one of her oldest, most reliable clients when the client hired a new employee who turned out to be an OCC.

Operating from her small home office, Diane turned out everything from business cards to magazines for a broad range of clients. Organized, detail-oriented, yet highly creative, she prided herself not only on the excellent quality of her work but also on her ability to finish most jobs ahead of deadline.

Over 10 years in business, Diane developed a sterling reputation, which eventually led to her having more work than she needed. This put her in the enviable position of being able to pick and choose her clients carefully, so she managed to avoid having "problem cases." That is, until Greg came along.

Greg was the new editor of a large church publication that Diane had designed and produced for several years. The church had been one of her best bread-and-butter clients, providing her with steady, reliable income. Greg's predecessor had been a delight to work with, always clear with directions and prompt about getting the newsletter copy to her on time. This was important, because Diane invariably set aside certain days and blocks of time to work on specific, recurring client projects. She expected her clients to respect her schedule as she respected theirs; and they did, giving her ample notice if they had to make any changes.

But Greg was a different story altogether.

Diane first sensed trouble when she noticed Greg wasn't returning her calls. She left him several messages to apprise him of her schedule and suggest possible times when they could meet either in person or by phone. Yet she got no response. Her concern mounted because she had several clients' projects to juggle and an upcoming trip planned.

Finally, after almost two weeks of silence, Greg left a message. His manner was pleasant, yet curiously he offered no excuses or apologies for his long delay in getting back to her. In fact, he made no reference to her messages at all. Diane was sure he had gotten them since she'd utilized both his voice mail and the church secretary.

Instead, Greg said only that he planned to fax her the edited copy "sometime soon—probably by the end of the week." (It was already Tuesday.) His vagueness and unconcerned air worried her.

Friday came and went with neither the promised fax nor any further communication from Greg. So she left him a message reminding him she was leaving town the following Friday. Late Monday morning, Diane left yet another message for Greg, stating politely that if she didn't receive the copy by 1:00 P.M. that day, there was no way she would have enough time to get the newsletter done before leaving on her trip. Five minutes later he called her back, and angrily accused her of being inflexible and unreasonable! She timidly reminded him that she'd left several messages for him, but he blatantly claimed he'd never gotten any messages from her, and even went so far as to say he didn't recall her ever saying anything about her impending trip.

Unused to this type of treatment and highly uncomfortable with confrontation anyway, Diane made little attempt to fight back.

Greg did fax her most of the copy by 1:00, and the remainder later. So, despite some problems, she was able to get the newsletter done on time. She told herself that since Greg was new on the job and had other duties at the church, perhaps she should have cut him some slack. Next month's newsletter process would no doubt go more smoothly, she hoped.

But instead, to Diane's dismay, the situation repeated itself. When she left messages or sent him faxes, he claimed he'd never received them. If she dropped something off at his office, he'd blame the secretaries for misplacing it.

After several months of this, Diane began to seriously consider ending her association with the publication. She hated to "fire" a good client, but she was afraid that dealing with Greg regularly might not be worth the stress.

Analysis:	OCC Client
OCC:	Greg
Chaos Category:	Communication-related
Chaos Specifics:	Doesn't return phone calls; does not communicate delays
Recommendations:	1) Stepping back 2) Referring 3) Clarifying

1. **Stepping back.** Before taking any kind of drastic action, it's wise to step back and try to visualize potential outcomes. There's an old saying: "Act in haste and repent at leisure." Remind yourself of that when you're faced with a difficult situation like Diane's.

Example: Diane made herself look at the big picture and came to the conclusion that Greg was destined to be only a temporary problem. Therefore, she decided not to let him ruin her relationship with what had been, until now, a good client. Instead, she resolved to work around him and do whatever was necessary to hang on until an opportunity for resolution presented itself.

2. **Referring.** From grade school on, we are socialized to believe that telling a higher-up about someone else's unacceptable behavior is tantamount to being a "snitch," a tattletale, a stool pigeon—in short, the lowest of the low. And it's true that people who make a habit of gossiping about others' failings and faux pas do not always engender respect. But there are times when, to resolve a problem situation that's beyond your control, you must refer it directly to someone's superior. So when you're not in a position to discipline someone whose chaos-causing ways are affecting your work, and you see no other way out, don't be afraid to speak up.

Example: Finally, Diane felt ready to come face-to-face with the problem instead of backing away from it. As luck would have it, her feeling of readiness coincided with a phone call from the church administrative director. He asked her how she liked working with Greg and if things were going okay.

Diane took this as a sign that perhaps others at the church were having difficulties with Greg, and she decided to be forthright and not hold back about describing his lack of professional behavior. She had always enjoyed a good rapport with the director, who knew her work and professionalism were above reproach.

To Diane's relief, the director thanked her for being so open and promised he would see to it that Greg would be handling things differently in the future. He also asked her to let him know if Greg presented any further problems.

3. **Clarifying.** Communicating in writing can help to clarify meaning by eliminating gaps and curbing misassumptions. It also provides a paper trail that may come in handy at a later point.

Example: Diane realized that speaking directly with Greg was not only uncomfortable but ineffective. (It was also uncommon, given his record for returning her phone calls.) So she resolved to communicate with him via fax only. Although it was a little more time-consuming than leaving voice mail messages, she found that it forced her to be extremely clear and specific—which left Greg no leeway for miscommunication excuses. Diane also kept a file of all her faxes to

Greg in case the occasion arose where she might need them as proof of her efforts and follow-through.

Diane never did find out exactly what the director said to Greg, but whatever it was, he managed to effect a dramatic turnaround in Greg's behavior. She also never actually spoke with Greg again, since he seemed to prefer using the fax as much as she did. Then, after only six months, he left, and his successor was someone Diane found much more pleasant to work with.

The OCC Boss

As the sole proprietor of a landscaping service, Hal had worked alone for many years. He was a fine gardener, knowledgeable and blessed with a proverbial green thumb. His customers loved him because he was both cheerful and reliable.

But eventually Hal's age began to catch up with him. Reluctantly he decided the time had come to get a helper, someone who could do the heavier work. He hired Chris, who was young, strong, and eager to learn about the landscaping business.

Chris got along well with Hal, but soon discovered that his new boss wasn't always easy to work with. For one thing, Hal was extremely disorganized. His pickup truck was a shambles, with gardening gear and gadgets jumbled together in no particular order. His tools seemed ancient and looked as though they'd never been cleaned or oiled, and some of his equipment was barely functional.

Worse, Hal's memory sometimes seemed as jumbled as his truck. (At first Chris worried that it might be Alzheimer's, but over time he came to realize Hal had always functioned this way.) He was always forgetting to bring along one special tool or another, and they'd have to drive all the way back to his garage to get it. Sometimes he forgot to bring gasoline for the gas-powered equipment they used; other times he'd forget to buy more fertilizer or pesticide. Whatever the cause, it invariably led to a special trip to purchase supplies, which meant they'd be running late for the rest of the day. Then Hal grumbled about having to pay his helper for the extra time, even though it wasn't Chris's fault.

And here was the worst part: Hal refused to admit that his own disorganization might be the key to all their delays. Because his truck was always in such a mess, it was impossible to see at a glance which tools and equipment he had loaded. And since there was no system for keeping track of supplies, he rarely knew when they were running low. In fact, it amazed Chris that Hal didn't mix up any of his jobs, since he never seemed to use any type of calendar or schedule. ("I keep'em all up here," he told Chris, tapping his balding head. "It's safer that way.")

Unfortunately, Hal got in the habit of blaming Chris for some of the problems. He complained that Chris "didn't put stuff back where it belonged," even though there was no way to tell where anything should go in his truck. Or he'd claim, for example, that Chris had used too much weed killer and that was why they were all out.

The last straw was when Hal tried to get out of paying Chris for the extra time. Chris realized he would have to either do something to improve the situation, or quit. And since he planned to eventually start his own landscaping business and was learning a lot about gardening from Hal, he didn't really want to quit.

Analysis:	OCC Boss
OCC:	Hal
Chaos Category:	Memory-related
Chaos Specifics:	Forgets to bring tools and replenish supplies
Recommendations:	1) Showing initiative 2) Systematizing 3) Maintaining

1. **Showing Initiative.** Quietly demonstrating your ability to get things organized is one of the best strategies for dealing with an OCC boss. Don't talk about it—just do it. Showing initiative can be an effective way to prove yourself while also improving your circumstances.

OCCs often have a lot of pride, which makes them particularly vulnerable to criticism. If they even sense you're judging them in any way, their hurt pride may cause them to lash out defensively. Therefore, the trick is to make changes without implying criticism of an OCC's original methods of operation. You want to be especially careful not to embarrass him. This will take tact, and a certain amount of craftiness on your part, but the results are worth it.

Example: Chris decided to get Hal's truck organized—on his own time. Figuring Hal might be insulted if he offered to do it, Chris thought up a way to get it done without a battle. He showed up an hour early one morning, telling Hal he'd had a fight with his girlfriend and had to get out of the house. Chris assured him there was no need to rush. "I'll be fine just hanging out in the truck," he told Hal. "Take your time; I'll get the equipment ready—no charge!"

Then Chris got to work. He pulled everything out of the back of the pickup, sorting as he went. He categorized hand tools, small gear, and supplies, using empty crates he'd brought along for that purpose, and arranged larger equipment in order of usage frequency. He grouped together all items in need of repair; got rid of the trash that had settled—like packing material—among the stuff; swept out the truck bed; and put everything back (except the trash).

By the time Hal came out of the house, Chris was sitting in the driver's seat, whistling and reading an old newspaper he'd discovered during his excavation. Hal stood still for a moment, looking over his newly organized truck. Then, without a word, he opened the door to the passenger side and got in. "Let's go," he said. "We've got a busy day." That was it. But that day was the first time they got all their jobs finished early. And Hal, still with no comment, paid Chris for his extra hour.

2. **Systematizing.** Creating easy-to-maintain systems is crucial to the process of getting anyone organized, and OCCs are no exception. Focus on the areas in which systems will make the most impact, and then go for it.

Example: Organizing Hal's truck got Chris thinking about other things he could do to get things in better order. He felt that having a system to keep track of supplies could save time by eliminating extra trips to the store. Chris created a checklist form with columns for all the different types of pesticides, weed killers, fertilizers, and other products Hal liked to use. Then he took the initiative and started monitoring the supplies. He began to let Hal know when they were starting to run low on any product, and he made sure they had sufficient quantities of any supplies that would be needed for all the jobs before they left each morning.

The form worked so well that Chris was inspired to make checklists for tools and equipment. Reviewing these in the morning with Hal virtually eliminated the problem of forgetting to bring along any special gear from Hal's toolshed.

3. **Anticipating.** You don't have to be clairvoyant to know how to antic-ipate potential problems—just organized. Organized people tend to think proactively. (The opposite is true for Chaos Creators, who exhibit classic reactive behavior, rushing to fix things after they have a prob-lem.) Anticipating chaos-bumps in the road helps you plan to avoid both pitfalls and pratfalls.

Example: Chris started arriving for work 10 minutes early. It gave him a chance to check over the gear and make sure everything was work-ing and in order; if something wasn't, he'd let Hal know so that they could plan the day accordingly.

Little by little, Chris's efforts had a positive effect, and work began to go much more smoothly. Hal never mentioned it—but he uncom-plainingly gave Chris a raise.

By helping his boss get organized without actually confronting him about his disorganization, Chris helped himself as well. And when Hal finally decided to sell his business and retire, guess who he sold it to?

The OCC Assistant

Alan worked as a benefits-plan adviser for a large insurance company. When he was promoted to manager of his department, he inherited his predecessor's secretary, Kim. Almost immediately, he began having problems with her.

The first thing that bothered Alan was Kim's desk. It was always piled high with bulging file folders and loose papers, and she seemed to spend a lot of time rooting around in the piles. When he made what he thought was a jocular comment about her "Swiss Alps of paper," Kim rewarded him with a cold stare. "I've got too much to do here and no time to keep it tidy," she complained. "And anyway, I know where every-thing is."

But "where everything is" turned out to be "here somewhere," as Alan discovered to his chagrin. Almost every time he asked Kim for a document, hours would pass before she could deliver it to him. Yet she always had an excuse for the delay and became very defensive if Alan questioned any of her alibis.

One day Kim was out sick. On a whim, Alan decided to take a closer look at her filing system. Opening the drawers, he was dismayed—but not surprised—to discover a hodgepodge of different-colored folders crammed together in semi-alphabetical order. It was a veritable jungle of disorganization.

Some of the labels were missing, but Alan could see where they'd fallen: the cracked plastic carcasses of old file tabs littered the drawer bottoms like crystalline beetles. Most of the folders were overstuffed, their innards bursting out the sides. Yet a few, perversely, were completely empty; no doubt the contents had been transferred, long ago, to the top of Kim's desk. Papers were even stuck between—not inside— several folders. All in all, it was not a pretty sight.

"No wonder so many of them are on her desk," he thought. "She can't fit them back in the drawers!"

Alan decided something had to be done about "Kim's Pile 'n' File Emporium" (as he had begun to privately refer to it). He realized the problem would keep getting worse if it wasn't addressed soon. Although he winced at the thought of confronting her, Alan resolved to plan a strategy for dealing with her after she returned.

Analysis:	OCC Assistant
OCC:	Kim
Chaos Category:	Information-related
Chaos Specifics:	Ineffective filing system; has difficulty locating documents
Recommendations:	1) Directing 2) Educating 3) Collaborating

1. **Directing.** Allowing a subordinate's defensive attitude to intimidate you is tantamount to giving away your power to effect change—not a wise choice. It's far more effective to demonstrate control of the situation by your attitude and actions.

One way to do this is to provide clear, consistent direction to your secretary or assistant. In other words, state specifically what you expect of him or her and by what date. Face the fact that having an assistant means you are the one in charge, and you must set the tone for the relationship. Directing is part of your job.

Example: Alan sat down with Kim and told her that the filing system had to be revamped so that he could locate files if she was not available. (He took care not to actually criticize her or her current filing methods.) He said that he knew it would be a major project so he was prepared to assist in several ways.

First, if Kim wanted to work on the project herself, he could authorize overtime pay. Alan would help with it, and/or he could bring in an organizing consultant (yours truly). If Kim was unable or unwilling to work overtime, Alan would handle the project along with the organizer.

After some discussion, Kim agreed to work with Alan on reorganizing the filing system. However, she didn't want to use an organizing consultant, unless the project turned out to be more than she had bargained for.

2. **Educating.** Don't assume that someone knows how to set up a filing system just because he or she works in an administrative position. Nowadays, many people employed as administrative assistants don't know the first thing about setting up or reorganizing paper systems, although they might be able to maintain a system that's already in place. Therefore, you may have to educate your secretary or assistant about the process. Options include workshops, organizing consultations, or books. (See Appendix A for recommendations.)

Example: Alan was able to get authorization for me to present an in-house workshop on filing systems which most of the support staff, including Kim, attended. Afterward, he heard excellent feedback. Kim even told him she was surprised at how helpful it had been. Gratified, he thanked Kim for her participation, and noted to himself that her defensiveness seemed to be receding.

3. **Collaborating.** Few worthwhile things are ever achieved without some type of collaborative process. Reorganizing a filing system is no exception. (See Chapter 6 for specific recommendations.) Working side-by-side with your assistant enables you to direct, delegate, and oversee the project, ensuring a more positive outcome.

Example: Using the instructions given at the workshop, Alan worked together with Kim to restructure the filing system. It took three exhausting Saturdays to complete it. But by the time they'd finished the project, not only was the system in better shape, they also had established a better working relationship.

After Alan overcame his initial reluctance to take charge "like a boss," he learned how to work with Kim more effectively. And as Kim developed more self-confidence through updated skills, her overall attitude improved.

The OCC Partner

Susan and Dennis were partners in business as well as in marriage. Together they ran a real estate sales office that was part of a major company. Overall, they worked well as a team, splitting duties equitably and balancing each other's strengths and weaknesses. Detail-oriented Dennis ran the office, handling the paperwork and the phones; "Schmoozin' Susan," as he liked to tease her, spent most of her time running around town, showing properties, and holding open houses.

The only bone of contention between them was what Dennis called Susan's "time problem." He just knew it was going to get them into deep trouble eventually. Susan did admit to "running a little late sometimes." But Dennis, a stickler for punctuality, claimed that it was more than "a little"—and a lot more than "sometimes." However, Susan argued that Dennis exaggerated and never gave her credit for all the times she was "only five minutes late."

They both agreed on one thing: Susan's schedule was pretty hectic. She was forever dashing from one end of town to the other, showing everything from big houses for sale to small rental units, and sandwiching an open house or two in between. When she wasn't talking with clients face-to-face, she was invariably on her cellular phone, especially while driving—or when stuck in traffic, as was often the case.

Susan considered running late an occupational hazard and felt it was no big deal. But Dennis believed that it showed a lack of professionalism. He also worried that Susan might lose a client if, for example, she showed up late to one of her open houses and ended up missing a potential buyer. It had almost happened on at least three separate occasions, as he often reminded her—much to her annoyance.

Finally, since Susan didn't really feel she had a problem, she told Dennis to either come up with a solution for her to try, or quit complaining.

Analysis: OCC Partner
Chaos Creator: Susan
Chaos Category: Time-related
Chaos Specifics: Late to appointments and meetings
Recommendations: 1) Caring 2) Scheduling 3) Reminding

1. **Caring.** Constantly harping on the problem creates negative feelings and may fuel resistance to solutions. Instead, try a softer approach, and show that you care more about the person than the problem.

Example: Dennis realized he was giving Susan the impression that all he cared about was having her be on time. Actually, his primary concern was for her health and safety. She was always overbooked and running behind schedule, rushing along while talking on her cell phone. He feared it was just a matter of time before she got in a car accident. He also worried that she was under too much stress.

Dennis decided to explain to her his underlying fears, and let her know that what he cared most about was her well-being. This was difficult for him because he wasn't used to expressing himself about "touchy-feely stuff," as he called it. But when he did, Susan was gratified and touched. And she became more open to his ideas about how they could make her schedule less hectic.

2. **Scheduling.** In certain occupations, effective scheduling is more of an art than a science. But no matter how complicated the schedule, it's important to always build in some Gap-Time to ensure at least a modicum of flexibility.

Example: Like many successful real estate salespeople, Susan tried to accommodate clients' schedules almost to the detriment of her own. But juggling too many back-to-back appointments was taking its toll—and occasionally backfiring.

Dennis suggested she schedule a few 20- to 30-minute break points (not breaking points) throughout the day to create shock absorbers for unplanned "schedule bumps," such as heavy traffic or late-running meetings with clients. Susan was willing to give the idea a try, and found—to her surprise—that it often prevented her from being late and also helped her feel less pressured.

3. **Reminding.** Products such as pagers and wristwatch alarms can be used to remind someone, "Time's up!" Audible tones (as opposed to vibrating mode) also convey an urgency, which can help cut short an appointment that may have dragged on into the "schmooze-and-lose" stage.

Example: Dennis offered to monitor Susan's schedule and remind her, via her pager, when it was time to wrap things up with one client so she could be on time for the next one.

Another option he suggested proved to be more realistic: each night he programmed her wristwatch alarm for the next day's appointments. Although Susan initially felt the alarm was somewhat intrusive, once she got used to it, she found that it did help her function more efficiently.

By softening his approach, Dennis was able to replace contentiousness with caring, which allowed Susan to get off the defensive and become more open to accepting help. And as with most business-marriage partnerships, the positive changes benefited their personal relationship as well.

General Advice for Coping with OCCs

1. Do not make blame an issue.
2. Be willing to let them take credit for improvements.
3. Never argue with their excuses; accept them and move on.

12

When Bureaucracy Cultivates Chaos:

ADVICE FOR BUREAUCRATIC CHAOS CREATORS

*A bureaucrat's idea of cleaning up his files is to
make a copy of every paper before he destroys it.*

—Dr. Laurence J. Peter

Remember that old expression, "It's more important to do the right thing than to do things right"? Unfortunately, Bureaucratic Chaos Creators (BCCs) do not understand this concept. For example, let's say a BCC has been assigned the task of painting a birdcage. He decides to spray-paint the cage without taking out the parrot. Technically, this is an efficient way to do the job; unfortunately for the parrot, however, it's not an effective way. The bird dies, but the job is completed to the BCC's satisfaction. Efficient but not effective—that's one way to describe BCCs.

You'd think their knack for efficiency would make BCCs strive for simplicity. But no. They have a way of complicating even the simplest task—for others. (Anything to make you go away so they can snack or doze in peace.) BCCs have an affinity for bureaucratic chaos tactics such as redundancy and red tape. They hate change; it takes energy and effort, and BCCs are basically lazy. Their mantra is, "It's always been done this way," and they blame the company culture for all chaos.

Not every BCC works in what you'd think of as a typical bureaucracy. But they do tend to gravitate toward inertia-rich work environments.

BUREAUCRATIC CHAOS CREATOR

BCC Traits Include . . .

◆ *Laziness.* BCCs will put out the smallest amount of effort possible to get any task or project done; efficiency is more important to them than effectiveness.

◆ *Inertia.* Because change involves effort, BCCs avoid it; changing anything (especially rules and policies) is too much work, even if it would eventually make things easier.

◆ *Apathy.* BCCs don't really care whether or not they're generating chaos, as long as it doesn't require much effort on their part.

Certain (dis)organizations provide a fertile breeding ground for their brand of chaos. BCCs attach themselves, remora-like, to the underbelly of a system—whether a government agency or a small company—and there they stay, steadily channeling chaos until they retire.

Unlike the other types of Chaos Creators, BCCs don't always generate chaos themselves; instead, they're likely to fan the flames of someone else's disaster. BCCs have an unparalleled gift for expanding the scope of the chaos generated by others. If you work with or have become a BCC, your challenges are monumental . . . but not necessarily insurmountable.

The BCC Boss

Julie, the fundraising director for a large nonprofit organization, was a self-proclaimed stickler for "doing everything by the book." Unfortunately for her assistant director, Lisa, she also wanted to keep revising "the book."

Though Lisa was kept more than busy doing all the nitty-gritty fundraising work such as event planning, direct-mail marketing, and endless phone solicitations, Julie still expected her to continuously write and rewrite sections for the policy and procedures manual that no one ever even opened.

Overall, Lisa didn't mind the workload; she liked her job and believed in the organization. She even took the optimistic view that the extra responsibilities were an opportunity to demonstrate her range of talents. What she did mind was the time she was forced to waste working with Julie on worthless documents. Julie insisted on meeting at least twice a week whether they needed to or not, and she was always running late. Lisa often had to sit outside her office for 15 or 20 minutes until Julie wrapped up whatever it was she was doing. Then when they finally did meet, she took her time going over each and every paragraph of the latest never-to-be-read report or document.

Lisa really enjoyed her work and her fellow employees, but working with Julie was driving her crazy. A colleague told her I might be able to offer her some suggestions on how to work better with Julie, so Lisa contacted me. She asked if I could help her figure out a way to keep both her sanity and her job. The plan I developed for Lisa helped her solve the problem *and* get ahead in her career.

Analysis:	BCC Boss
Chaos Creator:	Julie
Chaos Categories:	Time- and Information-related
Chaos Specifics:	Never prepared for meetings that she schedules
Recommendations:	1) Anticipating 2) Sitting back 3) Duplicating

1. **Anticipating.** Repeatedly experiencing the same problems with certain people in specific situations should teach you what to expect in your future dealings with them. By learning to anticipate chaos-causing activity, you'll be able to sidestep it.

Example: From past experience, Lisa knows what to expect from Julie and finally understands her M.O. Now she usually calls her boss a few minutes before their scheduled meeting time and claims to be running about 15 minutes late. This gives Julie the extra time she needs to prepare for the meeting, without inconveniencing Lisa.

Of course, Lisa doesn't employ this technique exclusively since she doesn't want Julie to catch on to her ruse.

2. **Sitting back.** Being proactive isn't always the best way of dealing with Chaos Creators, especially BCCs, who often thrive on nonaction themselves. Sitting back and just letting things happen is sometimes a valid option, and one that's often overlooked by hyperorganized, do-it-now types.

Try to recognize times when absence of action actually may be a more effective coping mechanism than proaction. "Practice not-doing, and everything will fall into place," wrote Lao-tzu, the venerable 6th century B.C. Chinese philosopher. So go ahead: sit back, relax—and see what happens. (I dare you!)

Example: Occasionally Lisa, already prepared for her meeting with Julie, just continues working at her desk until she gets a call asking her where she is. Julie's call signifies that she's finally ready; therefore, Lisa can go to her with some assurance that she won't be kept waiting or get sent away. However, Lisa makes sure not to overdo this technique either, knowing that Julie doesn't like to be kept waiting herself.

3. **Duplicating.** Since BCCs usually are comfortable with redundancy, it can work in your favor to exploit this tendency. Providing duplicate materials initially may seem wasteful, but it may save you time, and aggravation, in the long run.

Example: Memos, brochures, special mailing pieces, charts, vendor invoices, correspondence—these were just some of the types of paperwork that Julie received from Lisa regularly to keep her informed of what Lisa was doing. But since Julie rarely filed anything Lisa gave her, she invariably misplaced the materials she wanted to review during their "update meetings."

Lisa also created an "Update Meetings" folder for herself containing copies of any materials she had given Julie since their last session. Then she got the idea of setting up and maintaining a duplicate file to bring along to each meeting. When Julie inevitably started flailing around among her papers in search of one of Lisa's documents, Lisa would produce the duplicate file, saying, "Here are all the materials, so you don't have to bother looking for them." This tactic stopped Julie in her search and forced her to stay on track.

Lisa's ability to use bureaucratic tactics for her own benefit was highly effective. Eventually, Julie moved on to a higher position in another organization—and she recommended Lisa for her old job.

The BCC Coworker

(*Note:* I almost didn't include this case history because I thought it sounded too unbelievable. But it's true. It actually happened to the former coworker of a friend of mine.)

Sid was a full-time case worker for a government social services agency. At least, according to his paycheck he was full-time; but you couldn't prove it by his coworkers. As his increasingly annoyed colleagues knew, the actual amount of work he did was less than part-time. Sid appeared to view his job as a way to supplement his "real" work, as a real estate sales agent. His attitude as a social worker seemed to be, "Do the minimum and pick up the paycheck." But because he was disorganized, juggling the demands of two very different jobs was more than he could manage. Eventually, even doing the minimum proved too much for him.

As a case worker, one of Sid's main duties involved "field investigations"—visiting his "cases" in their homes to observe their living conditions and verify their claims. But gradually he'd gotten in the habit of doing most of his investigations by phone, to save himself the time of traveling around the county. Needless to say, this reduced the credibility of his reports. But Sid usually got around this problem by simply failing to file his reports.

You might think such ineptitude would get him fired quickly—but only if you'd never worked for a government agency. In reality, Sid knew how to play the bureaucracy like a banjo. Each month his boss would parcel out Sid's uncompleted case work to his resentful coworkers, invariably right at deadline time. Everyone grumbled at having to pick up the slack for Sid, but since this was a government agency, grumbling was part of the office culture, and no one was willing to take action.

Left unchecked, Sid's real hours decreased to the point that his true output dwindled to virtually nothing. Eventually, he rarely made any attempt to contact his cases and he never completed his project work. Meanwhile, he was driving around—in a state-owned vehicle, no less—showing properties to his real estate clients.

Finally, Maria, a fellow case worker, could stand it no longer. Sid's chaos-causing ways pushed her to the breaking point. A hard-working single mother, she had little time or patience for shirkers like Sid. She was sick of fielding complaints from his cases when he didn't show up for scheduled appointments, and tired of doing his work for him when she already had too many of her own cases to handle.

Reluctant as she was to be a whistle-blower, Maria nevertheless approached her supervisor to complain, only to be fed a classic bureaucratic excuse: "Confidentially, Maria, it's too hard to get someone like Sid fired from this agency—too much paperwork. Anyway, he'll shape up once his real estate business dies down."

Inwardly fuming, Maria resolved to find a way to get Sid fired—or at least transferred out of her department.

Analysis:	BCC Coworker
Chaos Creator:	Sid
Chaos Category:	Project-related
Chaos Specifics:	Doesn't do case work; misses deadlines
Recommendations:	1) Showing initiative 2) Researching
	3) Documenting

1. **Showing initiative.** One of the problems of working with BCCs is that your situation is often rooted in the miasma of a bureaucracy. Therefore, facilitating change by showing initiative can be tricky—even risky—unlike in the business world, where you can get ahead by demonstrating your moxie. Bureaucratic culture dictates blending in as opposed to sticking out; so therefore, show initiative quietly. Your reward most likely will be in the results attained, since you probably won't get any credit for achieving them.

Example: Maria decided to find out exactly what steps were needed for building a case against Sid. She knew there was some truth in what her supervisor had said; there was bound to be plenty of paperwork involved. But Maria was willing to do what had to be done. From a friend in another department, she learned where to locate the government procedures she'd have to follow. Then she got down to business.

2. **Researching.** When dealing with any bureaucracy it's important to work within the existing framework. (Unless you want to try to fight City Hall, so to speak.) Take the time to research procedures and rules that pertain to your situation. Daunting? Sometimes. Necessary? Always.

Example: Maria spent several of her lunch hours poring over government-garbled rules, red-tape–wrapped regulations, and picayune procedural processes just to find the correct, officially sanctioned format for getting someone fired. (She saw why her supervisor had backed away from it; "too much paperwork" was, alas, an understatement of the truth.) But once she'd done the research, she knew exactly how to proceed.

3. **Documenting.** Documentation is always important when pinning down BCCs. Different bureaucracies have different documenting requirements, so be sure to follow code. A simple Chaos Log may suffice, but probably not.

Example: To document Sid's shenanigans according to policy, Maria had to become virtually a one-woman surveillance squad for an entire month. She even bought a wig to disguise herself when following Sid around town. Like an amateur sleuth, she noted exactly where he went and when; she also listened in on some of his conversations at work. Of course, her own work suffered during the course of her surveillance, but she had arranged for two fellow case workers to help out; they were happy to, once they heard what she was up to.

At the end of the month, Maria had accumulated a binder full of documentation on Sid's whereabouts and doings, all kept according to code. She presented it to her supervisor, who subsequently arranged for a hearing for Sid. At the hearing, the evidence Maria had assembled proved more than adequate for Sid's dismissal.

Not only did Maria's sleuthing pay off, but it made her a hero among her coworkers. Plus, she learned something about taking initiative, which eventually helped her move up the bureaucratic ranks.

The BCC Subordinate

Zack, a legal assistant at a busy law firm, was organized and efficient. He did everything from running interference to running errands. One of his regular duties involved delivering litigation filings—petitions, complaints, summonses—to the superior court for processing.

Considering the size of the court bureaucracy, that part of his job usually went fairly smoothly. Then one day a problem surfaced in the form of a small sign stating, "Henceforth, all filings must be signed in BLACK INK ONLY. Signatures in blue ink will not be considered valid." Zack was stunned. He had a whole stack of documents that were suddenly invalid—and for no apparent purpose.

Trying to talk with Rita, the desk clerk, was of little use. She had long ago mastered the mumbo-jumbo language of catch-22. "It's not a new rule; we've just never enforced it before," was her explanation. When Zack pressed for details, she became defensive: "Don't blame me; the presiding judge ordered the sign."

Zack was incredulous. He had never heard of any "rule" specifying ink color for signatures on legal filings; something was fishy about Rita's claim. It occurred to him that perhaps she had deliberately misinterpreted the judge's instructions to suit her own purposes. He'd long suspected that Rita and the other clerks were overwhelmed by the volume of documents they were responsible for processing. Maybe she'd hit on a way to staunch the flow, at least temporarily, while all the legal assistants went scrambling to get their documents redone.

Determined to get to the bottom of this mystery, and to get his filings processed, Zack rushed back to work, formulating a plan of action as he hurried along.

Analysis: BCC Subordinate
Chaos Creator: Rita
Chaos Category: Communication-related
Chaos Specifics: Misinterprets instructions
Recommendations: 1) Collaborating   2) Researching
                     3) Smoothing

---

1. **Collaborating.** Especially when dealing with a hydra-headed bureaucracy, two heads are better than one. And if you are not in a position of power yourself, it's often wise to enlist the aid of someone else who is.

Example: The first thing Zack did when he got back to the office was to tell Jennifer, a senior partner, what was going on down at the superior court clerk's office. Outraged by his story, she agreed to help him get the situation turned around.

2. **Researching.** When something doesn't ring true it can mean that somewhere along the way, the truth got mangled. Depending on your situation, unearthing the root of the problem may mean simply scratching the surface—or it could take some deep digging. Sometimes a little research goes a long way toward clearing up a "misunderstanding."

Example: Jennifer, with Zack in tow, checked the superior court Local Rule Book and, as expected, found no rule such as Rita had claimed. Armed with this information, Zack and Jennifer headed back to the court clerk's prepared to do battle.

When they confronted Rita, she—like all good BCCs—passed the buck. "I didn't actually talk to the judge myself," she admitted. "My boss, the chief clerk, passed along his orders to me. You'll have to talk to him, and he's not here now."

Undeterred, Zack and Jennifer decided to track down the presiding judge himself. Luck was with them; they caught him just as he was heading out and regaled him (quickly) with the tale of the sign. Amazed, he told them what he'd really said to Rita's boss, the chief clerk: "I merely stated that I was sick of seeing illegible pleadings. I've found too many poor-quality photocopies filed as originals. That's all!"

Next, Zack and Jennifer managed to locate the chief clerk, who, when asked about the sign, seemed irritated. "Rita must have misunderstood my meaning. I told her that the judge wanted clearer copies of documents in the files. I don't know where she got the idea of banning blue-ink signatures," he sniffed. "I'll have to talk with her about that. In the meantime, we'll do something about the sign."

3. **Smoothing.** Once you've achieved your objective, don't press your advantage too hard or, worse, gloat about it. It's far wiser to be gracious about your victory. Make an obvious effort to smooth things over so that resentments are less likely to build up.

Example. Returning to the clerk's office, Zack and Jennifer cornered Rita and recounted their findings. But Zack, mindful of his future dealings with her, made a point of giving Rita an "out" by saying, "This whole escapade reminds me of the old game of Telephone! It just goes to show, verbal communication can be tricky."

Zack was wise enough to avoid attempting to deal with the bureaucracy on his own. By enlisting the help of a useful and sympathetic ally, he quickly and effectively derailed a potentially chaotic situation.

The BCC Assistant

Barry, the assistant manager of a large chain drugstore, had always gotten ahead by following the rules and doing things exactly the way they'd always been done. He was dependable and hard-working, routinely putting in 60-hour weeks. He took care of everything from shopping cart problems to shoplifters, always trying to do his best.

Despite all these good qualities, Barry had one fault that really frustrated his manager Jim: he was unable to stay focused, especially when things got hectic. Part of the reason for his distraction was related to his conscientiousness about following a company policy, the chain's "Golden Rule of Retail," which stated; "The Customer Comes First. Always stop whatever you're doing to help a customer."

Barry, however, took this rule to the extreme, and even when he was in the middle of helping one customer, would stop to help another. Then, he would often forget he was helping the first customer and would move on to another project. More than once Jim had gotten complaints from customers who had stood around waiting for Barry to return, only to see him stocking shelves or running a cash register.

Barry's memory problems were also causing problems with the employees. One Friday, he forgot Jim had told him to have the Summer Special Soda display put up at the front of the store. When the Pepsi truck arrived, Barry told the driver to just unload all the cartons into the back storeroom, rather than at the front. As a result, Jim had to pull several clerks from other assignments to move the boxes to the right spot.

Jim liked Barry, and didn't want to fire him. He knew Barry was, in general, a fine assistant manager—as long as he didn't have to handle more than one problem or task at a time.

Analysis:	BCC Assistant
Chaos Creator:	Barry
Chaos Category:	Memory-related
Chaos Specifics:	Forgets to return to interrupted tasks; forgets instructions
Recommendations:	1) Reminding 2) Assisting 3) Delegating

1. **Reminding.** Easily sidetracked Chaos Creators often need some type of reminding device or system to assist their memories and keep them on track. By recommending various methods (high-tech and low-tech), you can benefit—and so can they.

Example: Jim suggested to Barry that he experiment with two reminding options: either a clip-on stopwatch—set for two minutes—to remind him to get back to his previous task; or a small notepad with attached pen for jotting quick reminders. Taking just a few seconds to use the reminder system ensures calm instead of chaos, he pointed out.

Barry chose the notepad method. He found one that clipped onto his belt, and developed a personal shorthand for making super-quick notes. It took him a few weeks to get in the habit, but eventually he became comfortable with the process—and pleased with his improved memory.

2. **Assisting.** Providing assistance for a Chaos Creator who's in an assisting position might sound a bit, well, redundant. (Sort of like the clas-

sic bureaucratic conundrum about the Department of Redundancy Department.) Yet sometimes it's a necessary step, especially when dealing with Chaos Creators who don't function well under pressure: During particularly busy or stressful days or times, they're going to need recurring assistance. So it's useful to 1) identify exactly when they're most likely to cause chaos (you may need to use a Chaos Log), and 2) if possible, arrange for someone to assist them during those periods.

Example: Saturday afternoons were generally quite busy at the store. On those days, no matter how hard Barry tried, he still had problems juggling customer demands and other issues. Acknowledging that Barry needed some type of assistance during peak hours, Jim assigned a part-time stockroom clerk as the assistant manager's "tag-along." (The clerk Jim selected for the job was someone he was grooming for an eventual management position.) The tag-along's job initially involved keeping Barry on track by reminding him about previously interrupted tasks.

3. **Delegating.** Memory-challenged Chaos Creators free up their brain cells when they're able to delegate details to others. However, delegating doesn't come naturally to most people. Therefore, it's crucial to provide them with both the skills and the power to delegate. Be specific about granting permission to delegate; otherwise they may be unsure about whether—and how—to follow through.

Example: Jim encouraged Barry to develop more of a managerial approach by practicing delegation. Instead of trying to take care of everything himself, suggested Jim, why not delegate certain simple, specific tasks to his tag-along? Also, during slow periods, he could practice delegating minor jobs to other stockroom clerks or checkers.

At first, Barry was uncomfortable with the process. He feared people wouldn't like him if they thought he was trying to "boss them around." But over time, with Jim's coaching, he developed his own friendly, low-key style of delegating, and both he and Jim were gratified by the results.

Jim's willingness to help Barry work around his weaknesses eventually made both their jobs easier. (The tag-along clerk benefited too: his title was changed to Assistant Manager Trainee, and he went on to become a department manager.)

General Advice for Coping with BCCs

1. Practice thinking like a bureaucrat.
2. Whenever possible, enlist the help of others who are fed up with a BCC.
3. Work within the bounds of the bureaucracy—don't try to fight City Hall.

Epilogue

*The best effect of any book is that it excites
the reader to self activity.*
—Thomas Carlyle

*T*his book was written to inspire and motivate you to go out into the world and conquer chaos for yourself and others.

I hope you will use the strategies and tools presented in these pages to help you become a Chaos Conqueror. I hope, too, that you've been entertained as well as enlightened.

But at the very least, you now have a new and improved vocabulary with which to describe a variety of chaos-caused frustrations in your workplace. Just imagine—instead of complaining, "I work with a disorganized jerk who ignores my attempts to communicate with him, constantly causes chaos, and then blames me for everything that goes wrong," you can suavely state, "I have an OCC who generates communication-related chaos." You'll sound so much more efficient and professional. Of course, other people won't have the faintest idea what you're talking about unless they've read this book. So by all means encourage them to run out and purchase it immediately!

If you have any chaos horror stories—or success stories, especially after using my suggestions—I'd enjoy hearing from you. Any feedback on this book is appreciated as well. Please contact me at the address listed on page 244 (and be sure to include your mailing address, e-mail address, and/or fax number).

Appendix A

RECOMMENDED RESOURCES

The following resources are recommended to help you continue conquering chaos.

Books

Baker, Sunny, and Kim Baker. *The Complete Idiot's Guide to Project Management*. New York: Alpha Books, 1999.

Rosen, Mark. *Thank You for Being Such a Pain*. New York: Harmony, 1998.

Schechter, Harriet. *How to Become a Professional Organizer*. 1994. For ordering information, send a self-addressed, stamped envelope to The Miracle Worker, PMB 199, 3368 Governor Drive, San Diego, CA 92122.

Schlenger, Sunny, and Roberta Roesch. *How to Be Organized in Spite of Yourself*. New York: Signet, 1989.

Shook, Robert, and Eric Yaverbaum. *I'll Get Back to You: 156 Ways to Get People to Return Your Calls and Other Helpful Sales Tips*. New York: McGraw-Hill, 1996.

Silber, Lee. *Time Management for the Creative Person*. New York: Three Rivers Press, 1998.

Silver, Susan. *Organized to Be the Best!* 3rd ed. Los Angeles: Adams-Hall, 1995.

Catalogs

Day-Timers	(800) 225-5005
Franklin-Covey	(800) 654-1776
Hello Direct	(800) 444-3556
Hold Everything	(800) 421-2264
Paper Direct	(800) 272-7377
Reliable Home Office	(800) 735-4000
The Sharper Image	(800) 344-4444

Services

BHB Consulting Services La Jolla, California	(858) 551-8860 Bruce H. Breier
Cowan & Company Professional Organizing San Diego, California	(858) 451-2344 Donna Cowan
The Miracle Worker Organizing Service San Diego, California	(858) 581-1241 Harriet Schechter
Organization Plus® Menlo Park, California	(650) 328-7475 Sharon Kristensen Deméré
Positively Organized! Los Angeles, California	(310) 207-7799 Susan Silver
Schlenger Organizational Systems Fairlawn, New Jersey	(201) 791-2396 Sunny Schlenger
Space Organizers White Plains, New York	(914) 997-1434 Stephanie Schur

Products Mentioned in Part II

CATEGORY	PRODUCT	AVAILABILITY
Time management systems	Day-Timers; Franklin	Catalog
Electronic organizers	Casio Executive BOSS; Rolodex Pocket Electrodex; Sharp Wizard	Major electronics outlets
Recording devices	FlashBack Digital Recorder; Executive Voice Organizer	Hello Direct catalog
	Olympus V-90 Digital Recorder	www.olympus.com
Labeling systems	Avery Personal Label Printer	Paper Direct catalog
	Brother P-touch labeler Kroy Duratype labeler	major electronics outlets (800) 776-5769
Miscellaneous	HelloSet Pro Headset	Hello Direct catalog

Appendix B

TURN CHAOS INTO CASH:
HOW TO PROFIT FROM YOUR ORGANIZING SKILLS

Organize Your Way to a Raise

Do your own performance review, detailing your accomplishments for the past year and documenting how you've met the goals that had been laid out for you (or that you'd set for yourself). Don't let your career dangle by the naive notion that you'll receive the credit you deserve for everything you've done for your company.

Organize Your Way to a Promotion

Show initiative. If your company doesn't have a procedures manual, create one—on your own time. If you work for a very large corporation, that may be too huge a project; instead, create guidelines for your own department. If there's already a procedures manual or guidelines but they're woefully inadequate or out of date, take it upon yourself to update and improve them. Again, do this on you own time so your job performance doesn't suffer.

Even though it could take you months to complete it, avoid discussing your project with anyone. Once you've finished, write a brief memo or letter explaining what you've done and why; then present it, along with the binder containing the manual or guidelines, to your immediate supervisor and the company chairperson or other head honcho.

Organize Your Way to a New Career

I was born an organized person; over the years I evolved into a Chaos Conqueror. It all started with my messy older sister, whose bedroom I was forced to share: I *had* to get it organized. (Not that she ever appreciated it.) Yes, even as a tiny, charming child, I had the power to create order out of chaos—and I knew how to use that power.

I progressed to helping my friends organize everything from their disorderly dollhouses to their cluttered closets. Helping others make their lives easier made me happy.

During college, my time management talents helped me earn my B.A. in record time, at the age of 19. After graduating, I honed my organizing skills in a variety of jobs; over time (and often overtime), my chaos-conquering abilities evolved to where I was actually helping people to become better organized themselves. This was more challenging than just organizing things for them, but also more rewarding. My metamorphosis from organized person to Chaos Conqueror had begun.

Eventually I became an editor. Editing is actually a form of organizing—it involves finding the right places for words, and knowing which ones to keep and which to get rid of. So in a way, it wasn't that big a leap for me to go from editing words to editing time and space. Five years after I became an editor, I made that leap, and The Miracle Worker was born. I had become a Chaos Conqueror—and a professional organizer.

You, too, can become a professional organizer. Moonlighting in your own business can bring you in extra cash while you're waiting for that raise or promotion to come through. Organizers usually charge from $25 to $125 per hour, depending upon expertise and locale. If you have bookkeeping and/or computer skills to supplement your organizing talents, you'll have ample opportunities to make good money working with clients on the weekends or even in the evenings, depending on your availability and energy level. (To find out more, see For Additional Help, page 244.)

For Additional Help

Harriet Schechter helps individuals and businesses conquer chaos through her customized consulting programs, seminars, and workshops. She also offers training for people who are interested in becoming professional organizers.

For information about her consulting and presentation programs, please visit her Web site at www.miracleorganizing.com; or write to The Miracle Worker Organizing Service, PMB 199, 3368 Governor Drive, San Diego, California 92122.

If you would like to receive information on how to become a professional organizer, send a stamped, self-addressed business envelope to the above address.

Acknowledgments

*I would maintain that thanks are the highest
form of thought; and that gratitude is
happiness doubled by wonder.*

—G. K. CHESTERTON

I am so very grateful to everyone who helped me with this project. Many people contributed in many different ways.

First I want to especially thank three who were truly invaluable during the sometimes chaotic process of creating this book:

My editor, Cherise Grant, whose amazing vision, ideas, suggestions, support, and enthusiasm for this project transformed it into something much bigger and better than I ever could have imagined.

My very own Miracle Worker, Marcia Richardson, whose creative talents, cheerful attitude, and unparalleled eye for detail made it possible for me to get this done!

My husband, Henry J. Marx, who contributed so much and in so many ways—insights, anecdotes, and feedback; meals, hugs, and chocolate; time, space, and quiet; unwavering faith, love, and spirit; and perhaps most important . . . my publicity photos.

Others who deserve extra-special mention:

Sharon Kristensen Deméré, whose knowledge of project management is surpassed only by her incredible generosity of spirit, and whose contributions to this book are too numerous to detail but are deeply appreciated.

T. R. Fleischer, whose loyal support and helpful input are indescribable and irreplaceable.

Bridget Hanley, whose thought-provoking observations never cease to both delight and enlighten.

Bella Silverstein, whose humorous illustrations enliven these pages, and who always manages to come through for me no matter what part of the world she's living in.

I would also like to thank the following who contributed both attributed and unattributed material: Bruce Breier, Donna Cowan, Dale Fetherling, Vicki T. Gibbs, Ruth Klampert, and Ruth Williams. And although I can't mention them by name, thanks to all my wonderful clients and seminar attendees.

Additional thanks to everyone at the Margret McBride Literary Agency, especially Kim, Kris, Donna, Sangeeta, and, of course, Margret herself. And special thanks to Jason Cabassi.

Thanks, too, to everyone at Simon & Schuster who helped to make this book a reality, including Mark Gompertz, Trish Todd, and Isolde Sauer. The efforts of copy editor Martha Cameron and Judy Wingerter from Pagesetters Inc. who designed the interior are also acknowledged.

I appreciate the love and support of all my friends—you know who you are.

Last but not least, I wish to thank my family. The assistance of my brother, Stuart, has been particularly helpful at various times during the years, and he deserves special praise. My sister, Janet, has provided inspiration and ideas to me for as long as I can remember and is also the bravest person I know. Her family—Stan, Louis, and Irene—help to light up my life. And our parents—well, this book is dedicated to them.

During the time this book was being created, my beloved father-in-law, Henry P. Marx, passed away. He is greatly missed.

Index